KU-548-778

ENGLISH

BERNARD HARTLEY & PETER VINEY

DEPARTURES

An intensive English course for beginners
Student's Edition

Oxford University Press

Oxford University Press
Walton Street, Oxford OX2 6DP

Oxford   New York   Toronto
Petaling Jaya   Singapore   Hong Kong   Tokyo
Delhi   Bombay   Calcutta   Madras   Karachi
Nairobi   Dar es Salaam   Cape Town
Melbourne   Auckland

and associated companies in

Berlin   Ibadan

Oxford and *Oxford English* are trade marks of
Oxford University Press

ISBN 0 19 432221 1 (student's edition)
ISBN 0 19 432222 X (teacher's edition)
ISBN 0 19 432225 4 (cassette)

© Bernard Hartley and Peter Viney 1978
First published 1978
Thirty-third impression 1992

This book is sold subject to the condition
that it shall not, by way of trade or
otherwise, be lent, re-sold, hired out, or
otherwise circulated without the
publisher's prior consent in any form of
binding or cover other than that in which
it is published and without a similar
condition including this condition being
imposed on the subsequent purchaser.

All rights reserved. No part of this
publication may be reproduced, stored in
a retrieval system, or transmitted, in any
form or by any means, electronic,
mechanical, photocopying, recording or
otherwise, without the prior permission
of Oxford Univerity Press.

Illustrations by:

David Ace   Michael Brownlow
Alun Burton   David English
Paddy Mounter   The Parkway Group
Jill Watkins

Photographs by:

Billett Potter

*The publishers would like to thank the
following for their time and assistance:*

Roy Ackerman Associates   Laura Ashley
British Rail   Browns Restaurant   City of
Oxford Motor Services   Debenhams Ltd.
Jem-i-ni   Oasis Trading   Post Office
Telecommunications   Radio Taxis
Randolph Hotel, Oxford   A. Woodward.

Printed in Hong Kong

The authors would like to thank all the people who helped in the development of this book. In particular we are grateful to the Directors of the Anglo-Continental Educational Group, and Chris Goodchild, Director of Studies, Anglo-Continental School of English, Bournemouth, for all their support and encouragement. We also wish to thank all our colleagues in the ACEG schools who provided invaluable comments and criticism.

Students can buy a cassette which contains a recording of the texts and dialogues in this book.

1 Hello

Exercise 1

David Clark
Linda Martin ·

Alan Smith
Susan Smith

John Green
Carol Green

He's David Clark.
She's Linda Martin.

· · · ·

· · · ·

Exercise 2

Is she a teacher?
No, she isn't.
Is she a student?
Yes, she is.

· · · a student?
No, · · ·
· · · a teacher?
Yes, · · · ·

Exercise 3

Is he from
 England?
No, he isn't.
Where's he from?
He's from Canada.

. . . Canada?
No, ...
. . . ?
. . . France.

. . . France?
. . . .
. . . ?
. . . Japan.

Exercise 4

Are you a teacher?
. . . .
Are you a student?
. . . .
Are you from
 England?
. . . .
Where are you
 from?
. . . .

2 Excuse me!

I Excuse me!
J Yes?
I Are you English?
J Pardon?
I Are you English?
J Oh, yes. Yes, we are.
I Oh, I'm English. Are you on holiday?
J No, we aren't. We're businessmen.

J Please, sit down . . .
I Thank you.

J Tea?
I Yes, please.

J Sugar?
I No, thanks.

J Where are you from?
I I'm from London.
J Are you a businessman?
I No, I'm not. I'm a tourist.

Where are you from?

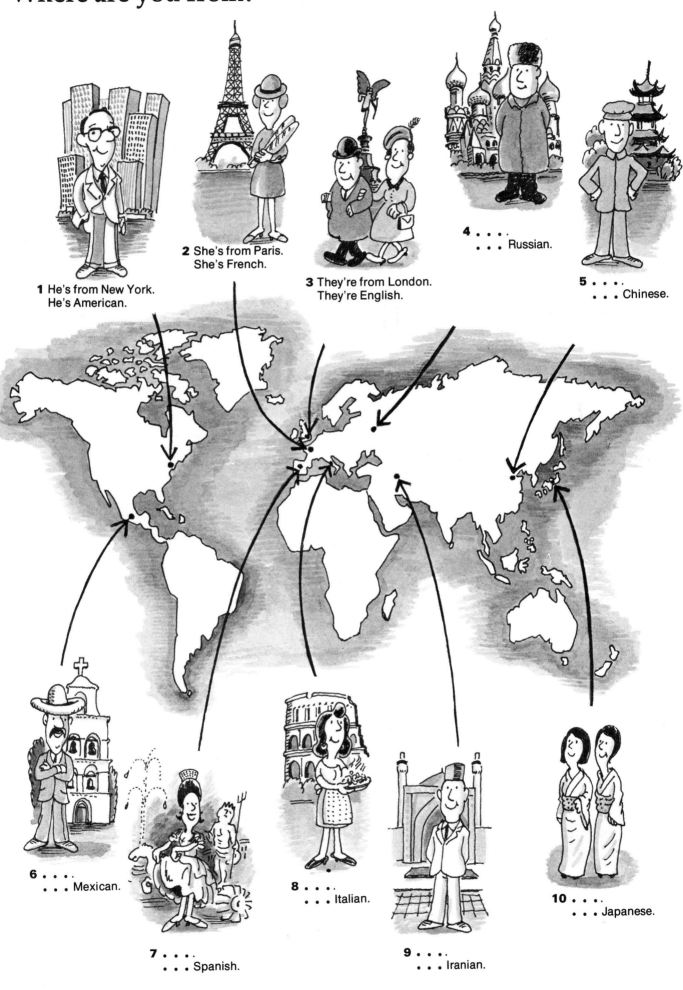

1 He's from New York. He's American.

2 She's from Paris. She's French.

3 They're from London. They're English.

4 . . . . Russian.

5 . . . . Chinese.

6 . . . . Mexican.

7 . . . . Spanish.

8 . . . . Italian.

9 . . . . Iranian.

10 . . . . Japanese.

3 What is it?

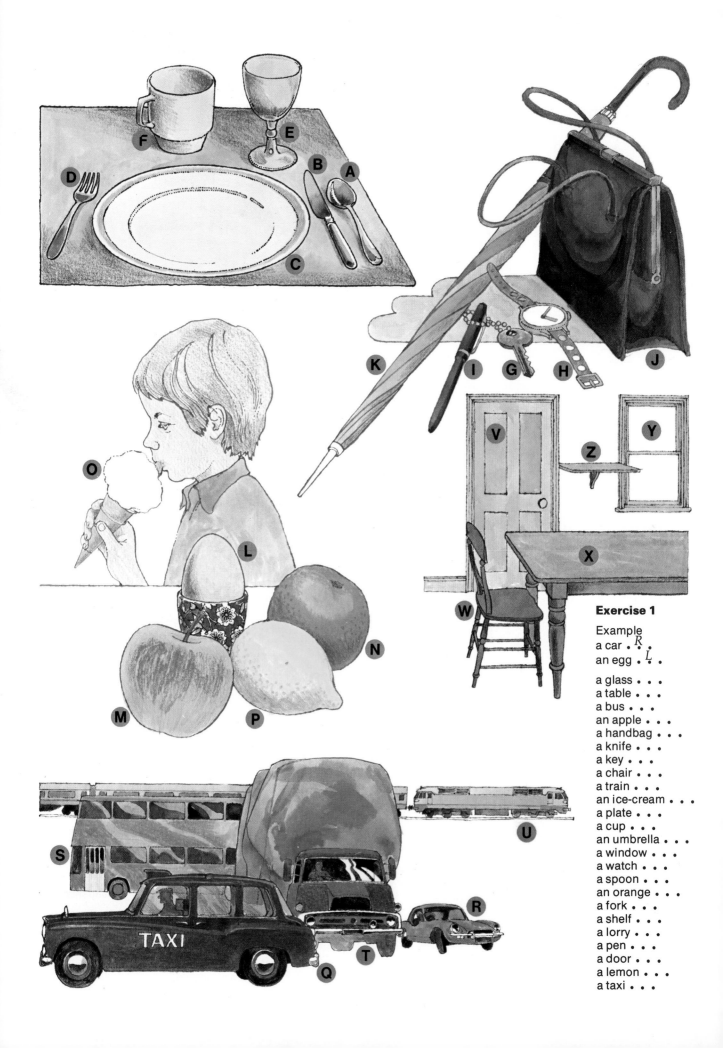

Exercise 1

Example
a car . *R* .
an egg . *L* .

a glass . . .
a table . . .
a bus . . .
an apple . . .
a handbag . . .
a knife . . .
a key . . .
a chair . . .
a train . . .
an ice-cream . . .
a plate . . .
a cup . . .
an umbrella . . .
a window . . .
a watch . . .
a spoon . . .
an orange . . .
a fork . . .
a shelf . . .
a lorry . . .
a pen . . .
a door . . .
a lemon . . .
a taxi . . .

What are they?

Exercise 2

1 They're forks.
2 . . . .
3 . . . .
4 . . . .
5 . . . .
6 . . . .
7 . . . .
8 . . . .

Use these words:
watches
cups
knives
keys
lorries
cars
glasses

Exercise 3

1 What is it?
It's a clock.

2 What are they?
They're radios.

3 . . . ?
. . . ashtray.

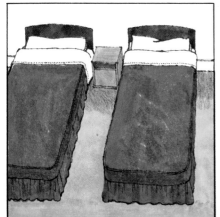

4 . . . ?
. . . beds.

5 . . . ?
. . . houses.

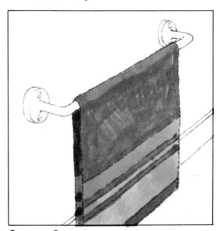

6 . . . ?
. . . towel.

4 What's your name?

Mr Dean Good evening.

Receptionist Good evening, sir. What's your name, please?

Mr Dean My name's Dean.

Receptionist Ah, yes . . . Mr Dean . . . Room 15. Here's your key.

Mr Dean Thank you.

Porter Is this your case?

Mr Dean No, it isn't.

Porter Oh, is that your case over there?

Mr Dean Yes, it is.

Mr Brown Good evening.

Receptionist Good evening. What are your names, please?

Mr Brown Mr and Mrs Brown.

Receptionist Ah, yes . . . here's your key.

Porter Are these your cases here?

Mr Brown No, they aren't.

Porter Oh, I'm sorry. Are those your cases over there?

Mr Brown Yes, they are.

Mrs Brown Is this our room?

Mr Brown What's the number?

Mrs Brown 14.

Mr Brown Oh, no, it isn't. That's our room . . . number 13.

What's your job?

Exercise 1

Look at 13.
What's his job?
He's a manager.

Look at 14.
What's her job?
She's a receptionist.

Look at 15.
What are their jobs?
They're waiters.

Look at 16.
• • •?
• • • •

Look at 17.
• • •?
• • • •

Look at 18.
• • •?
• • • •

Look at 19.
• • •?
• • • •

Use these words:

cleaners
cook
secretary
porter

Exercise 2

Look at 20.
What's his job?
He's a pilot.

21 • • •?
• • • •

22 • • •?
• • • •

23 • • •?
• • • •

24 • • •?
• • • •

Use these words:

pilot
policemen
air-hostess
taxi driver
mechanic

Exercise 3

What's your name?
• • • •
What's your job?
• • • •

5 I'm cold

A Ooh! I'm cold!
B Are you?
A Yes, I am.
B Oh, I'm not. I'm hot!

C *It's big.* **D** *It's small.*

E . . . . **F** . . . .

G . . . . **H** . . . .

I . . . . **J** . . . .

K . . . . **L** . . . .

M . . . . **N** . . . .

O . . . . **P** . . . .

Q . . . . **R** . . . .

S . . . . **T** . . . .

U . . . . **V** . . . .

W . . . . **X** . . . .

Y . . . . **Z** . . . .

Use these words:

	full	old	tall	strong	beautiful
	empty	new	short	weak	ugly
rich	thick	cheap	fat	old	long
poor	thin	expensive	thin	young	short

Exercise 1

Helen Wilson's *thirsty.*
Alan Wilson . . . .
Mrs Wilson . . . .
Miss Cook . . . .
Mr Parker . . . .
Mr Cooper . . . .
Mr West
and Mr Spencer . . . .

sad
angry
hungry
thirsty
tired
cold
hot

BIG JOE FREEZER-125 kilos
STEVE KING-68 kilos

Mrs Loot   Fred Penny

Exercise 2

Look at Steve King.   Now write four sentences for:

He's weak.   **a** Big Joe Freezer
He's small.   *He's heavy.*
He's light.   **b** Mrs Loot
He's thin.   **c** Fred Penny
He's young.

6 A nice flat

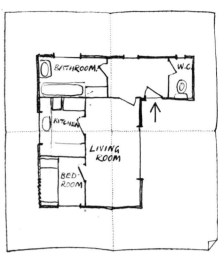

Agent This is a nice flat, Miss Wilkins. Here's a plan . . .
Miss Wilkins Mmm . . .
Agent There's a living-room. There's a kitchen, a bedroom, a bathroom, and there's a toilet.
Miss Wilkins Is there a balcony?
Agent No, there isn't.
Miss Wilkins . . . and a telephone?
Agent No, there isn't a telephone.

Agent Well here's the kitchen.
Miss Wilkins Hmm . . . it's very small.
Agent Yes, it isn't very large, but there's a cooker and a fridge. There are some cupboards under the sink.
Miss Wilkins Are there any plates?
Agent Yes, there are.
Miss Wilkins Good. Are there any chairs in here?
Agent No, there aren't, but there are some in the living-room.
Miss Wilkins Hmm. There aren't any glasses!
Agent Yes, there are! They're in the cupboard.
Miss Wilkins . . . and . . . er . . . where's the toilet?

Exercise 1

sofa
There's a sofa *in the living-room.*
radio
There isn't a radio *in the living-room.*

Write sentences with:
1 telephone   **3** cupboard
2 chair   **4** table

Exercise 2

books
There are some books *on the shelf.*
cups
There aren't any cups *on the shelf.*

Write sentences with:
1 glasses   **3** magazines
2 records   **4** bottles

Exercise 3

magazine/table?
Is there a magazine *on the* table?
books/shelf?
Are there any books *on the* shelf?

Write questions with:
1 radio/shelf
2 bottles/table
3 records/table

Exercise 4

Where are the bottles? They're on the shelf.
Where's the chair? It's in the living-room.

Answer the questions:
1 Where's the television?
2 Where are the glasses?
3 Where are the books?
4 Where's the sofa?

7 Everyday Conversation

A Excuse me.
B Yes?
A Is there a post office near here?
B Yes, there is.
A Is it far?
B No, it isn't very far. First right, second left.
A Thank you very much.
B That's all right.

post office
bus stop
bank
café
telephone box
supermarket

first
second
third

C Mrs Connor, could you pass the salt please?
D Certainly.
C Thank you very much.
D And the pepper?
C No, thank you.

salt
sugar
bread
vinegar

pepper?
milk?
butter?
oil?

E Good evening.
F Good evening.
E Half of bitter, please.
F Here you are, sir.
E Thank you very much. How much is that?
F 15p.

a pint
half a pint
a whisky
a double whisky

with lemon
with soda
with Coke

10p
£1.15
£1.50

G Are you on the phone?
H Yes, I am.
G What's your number?
H 23306

23306
66880
087432
72258
10443
90537
47925

Mrs Turner Who's that? Who's that?

Tom It's me . . . Tom.

Mrs Turner Tom?

Tom Yes, Tom . . . your grandson, . . . from Canada!

Mrs Turner Oh, Tom! Come in!

Tom This is my wife, Mary.

Mrs Turner Oh, how do you do?

Tom . . . and these are our children, Jimmy and Ethel.

Mrs Turner Hello, Jimmy. Hello, Ethel. Well, this is a nice surprise!

Look at Mrs Turner. Her skirt's black.
Her blouse is white.
Look at Tom. His jacket's brown.
His trousers are grey.
Look at Mary. Her dress is pink.
Her shoes are orange.
Look at Jimmy. His shirt's red.
His shorts are green.
Look at Ethel. Her T-shirt's yellow.
Her jeans are blue.

Exercise 1

Who's this?
It's Captain Adams.
He's an astronaut.

Captain Adams

Mrs Martin   Miss Prim   Dr Clark   Mr Smith
Use these words: housewife/policeman/secretary/doctor

Exercise 2

What colour is it?
It's red.

What colour are they?
They're blue.

9 Whose is it?

Richard Hello, Jane.
Jane Hello, Richard.
Richard Phew! What's this?
Jane It's a Cadillac.
Richard Hmm. Is it your car?
Jane Well, no . . . no, it isn't.
Richard Whose car is it?
Jane It's Mr Orson's car.
Richard Mr Orson? Who's he?
Jane He's my boss. He's a
millionaire!

1
2
3
4
5
6
7
8
9
10
11
12

Exercise 1

Who is it? It's Mr Orson.
Write sentences for B and C.

Exercise 2

1 *What is it? It's a cigar.*
2 *What are they? They're glasses.*
Write sentences for 3-12.

Exercise 3

1 *Whose cigar is it?*
It's Mr Orson's cigar.
2 *Whose glasses are they?*
They're Jane's glasses.
Write sentences for 3-12.

Look at this

Look at Dick:
He's Anne's husband.
He's Mike's father.

Look at Anne:
She's Dick's wife.
She's Sue's mother.

Look at Mike:
He's their son.
He's Sue's brother.

Look at Sue:
She's their daughter.
She's Mike's sister.

10 Is there any wine in the bottle?

There's some rice in the jar.
There's some milk in the bottle.
There's some sugar in the jar.
There's some oil in the bottle.
There's some water in the jug.
There's some wine in the bottle.

There are some apples on the table.
There are some eggs on the table.
There are some oranges on the table.
There are some bananas on the table.
There are some lemons on the table.
There are some onions on the table.

Exercise

butter

A *There's some butter in the freezer.*
B *How much is there?*
A *There's a lot.*

Write conversations with:
ice-cream
meat

There isn't any butter.

There isn't any cheese.

There isn't any beer.

There aren't any tomatoes.

There aren't any mushrooms.

There aren't any eggs.

The fridge is empty!

Is there any cheese in the fridge?
Yes, there is.

Is there any butter in the fridge?
No, there isn't.

Are there any eggs in the fridge?
Yes, there are.

Are there any tomatoes in the fridge?
No, there aren't.

hamburgers

A *There are some hamburgers in the freezer.*
B *How many are there?*
A *There are a lot.*

Write conversations with:
peas
chickens

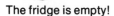

11 An English Restaurant

Customer Waiter! I'd like the menu, please.
Waiter Here you are, sir.
Customer Thanks . . . I'd like some soup . . . .
Waiter Tomato soup?
Customer Yes, please . . . and I'd like a steak.
Waiter Rare, medium, or well-done?
Customer Medium, please.
Waiter Which vegetables would you like?
Customer I'd like some potatoes, some peas, and a salad, please.
Waiter Certainly, sir.
Customer Oh, and I'd like some wine.
Waiter Which wine would you like, sir?
Customer A bottle of red wine, please.

MENU

Starters
Soup 60p
Fruit Juice 30p

Main Courses
Steak £3.40
Roast Beef £2.50
Chicken Casserole £2.60
Grilled Lamb Chops £2.70
Fried Plaice £2.80
Cheese Omelette £1.90

Vegetables
Chips 50p
Boiled Potatoes 50p
Peas 50p
Carrots 50p
Mushrooms 50p
Mixed Salad 70p

Desserts
Ice Cream
Apple Pie
Fruit Salad 50p
Cheese & Biscuits 40p

Drinks
Coffee 60p
Tea 70p
Milk

Wines (per bottle)
French Red 40p
Spanish White 30p
German White 20p
Italian White £3.20
Portuguese Rosé £2.90
                          £3.10
Service 10% £2.80
V.A.T. 15% £3.00

12 Do this! Don't do that!

Look at these pictures.

Charles Orson is a film director.
He's in the studio. He's with Steve
Newman and Raquel Evans.
Steve's an actor. Raquel's an
actress. They're film stars.

"Everybody! Be quiet, please!
O.K., Steve, now open the door
. . . come in . . . walk to the sofa
. . . . Walk! Don't run! . . . O.K.,
sit down . . . don't move . . . now,
take Raquel's hand . . . look into
her eyes . . . don't laugh! . . .
smile!
   Raquel! Smile at Steve . . . look
into his eyes . . . don't laugh! . . .
now, close your eyes. Steve! Kiss
her! That's fine! Now, Steve, go to
the door . . . go out, and close the
door . . . O.K., turn the lights on
. . . turn the microphones on . . .
start the camera . . . action!"

Exercise

13 Elton Kash

Look at this man.
He's Elton Kash.
He's a pop star.
He's very rich and famous.
Look at his house.
It's large and expensive, and
there's a swimming-pool in the
garden.
There are ten bedrooms in the
house.
Elton's car's American.
It's a 1978 Lincoln Continental.
It's fast and comfortable.
In his car there's a radio, a stereo
cassette-player, a cocktail cabinet,
a cigar lighter and electric
windows.
But Elton isn't happy . . . he'd like
a Rolls-Royce.

Look at this man.
He's Mr Wilson.
He's a teacher.
He's very poor and he isn't
famous.
Look at his house.
It's small and cheap and there isn't
a garden.
There are only two bedrooms in
the house.
Mr Wilson's car's English.
It's a 1959 Mini.
It's slow and uncomfortable.
In his car there isn't a radio or a
cassette-player . . . there's an
engine, a steering-wheel, and
there are four wheels and two
doors.
Mr Wilson isn't happy . . . he'd
like a new Mini.

Exercise

Elton's a pop star. Mr Wilson's a teacher.

Elton's rich.   • . . .
Elton's car's American.   • . . .
Elton's house is large
  and expensive.   • . . .
He'd like a Rolls-Royce.   • . . .

14 At the hairdresser's

Jane . . . Oh, yes, my husband's wonderful!

Sally Really? Is he?

Jane Yes, he's big, strong and handsome!

Sally Well, my husband isn't very big, or very strong . . . but he's very intelligent.

Jane Intelligent?

Sally Yes, he can speak six languages.

Jane Can he? Which languages can he speak?

Sally He can speak French, Spanish, Italian, German, Arabic and Japanese.

Jane Oh! . . . My husband's very athletic.

Sally Athletic?

Jane Yes, he can swim, ski, play football, cricket and rugby . . .

Sally Can he cook?

Jane Pardon?

Sally Can your husband cook? My husband can't play sports . . . but he's an excellent cook.

Jane Is he?

Sally Yes, and he can sew, and iron . . . he's a very good husband.

Jane Really? Is he English?

Questions

1 Is Jane's husband big?
2 Is he ugly?
3 Can he play football?
4 Can he speak French?
5 Can he ski?
6 Can he sew?
7 Is Sally's husband athletic?
8 Is he intelligent?
9 Can he speak Arabic?
10 Can he play cricket?
11 Can he play rugby?
12 Can he iron?

Exercise

Example:
I can drive.
I can't swim.

Write ten sentences.

15 Everyday Conversation

I Please come in.
J Thank you.
I Please, . . . sit down. Would you like a cup of tea?
J Yes, please.
I How about a biscuit?
J No, thanks. I'm on a diet.

a cup of tea
a cup of coffee
a glass of milk
a glass of beer
a glass of water

a biscuit
a sandwich
a piece of cake
an orange
a chocolate

K Excuse me . . .
L Yes, Can I help you?
K Yes, I'd like some information about trains please.
L Where to?
K . . . to London.
L When?
K Tomorrow.
L Morning or afternoon?
K In the evening. About six o'clock.
L There's one at 6.40.
K Thank you.

trains
buses
planes
boats
excursions

M I'd like a pair of shoes, please.
N What colour would you like?
M Brown.
N And what size are you?
M Five. Can I try them on?
N Of course.

a pair of shoes
a raincoat
a pullover
a cardigan
a pair of jeans

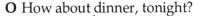

O How about dinner, tonight?
P I'd love to.
O Where can we meet?
P How about the square?
O All right. What time?
P Is seven o'clock OK?
O Yes, that's fine.

dinner
a film
a walk
a concert
a drink

16 Gloria Gusto, Tom Atkins and Terry Archer

Hi, there! My name's Gloria Gusto.
I'm an actress.
I'm from London.
I've got a flat in London and a house in Hollywood, with a swimming pool.
I've got a new Rolls-Royce and a lot of money in the bank.
I've got a husband, and three wonderful children in Hollywood.
Life's great!
I've got everything!

Hello, my name's Tom Atkins.
I'm from London, too.
I'm broke. I haven't got any money.
I haven't got a job or a house, or a car.
I haven't got a wife, and I haven't got any children.
Life's terrible!
I haven't got anything!

Look at this man.
His name's Terry Archer.
He isn't from London.
He's from Oxford.
He's a factory worker.
He's got a good job.
He's got a car.
He hasn't got a big house, he's got a flat.
He's got a wife, but he hasn't got any children.
Life's all right.

Exercise 1

Example: flat in London
Has she got a flat in London? *Yes, she has.*

1 house in Hollywood.
2 swimming-pool.
3 Rolls-Royce.
4 lot of money.
5 husband.
6 three children.

Exercise 2

Example: a job
Has he got a job? *No, he hasn't.*

1 a house.
2 a car.
3 a wife.
4 any money.
5 any children.

Questions

1 What's his name?
2 Where's he from?
3 What's his job?
4 Has he got a good job?
5 Has he got a car?
6 Has he got a flat or a house?
7 Has he got a wife?
8 Has he got any children?

Exercise 3

Example:
brother   *I've got a* brother.
Rolls-Royce *I haven't got a* Rolls-Royce.

Write four sentences:
1 watch   3 bicycle
2 sister   4 umbrella

17 At the customs

Customs Officer Good morning. Can I see your passport?

Man Certainly. Here it is.

C.O. Yes, that's all right. Have you got anything to declare?

Man Yes, I have.

C.O. What have you got?

Man I've got some whisky and some cigarettes.

C.O. How much whisky have you got?

Man A litre.

C.O. That's all right. And how many cigarettes have you got?

Man Two hundred.

C.O. Fine. What about perfume? Have you got any perfume?

Man Er . . . No, I haven't.

C.O. Good. Open your case, please.

Man Pardon?

C.O. Open your case, please. Open it now! Oh, dear! Look at this! You've got three bottles of whisky, four hundred cigarettes and a lot of perfume!

Questions

1 Has he got anything to declare?
2 Has he got any cigarettes?
3 Ask "How many?"
4 Has he got any perfume?
5 Ask "How much?"
6 Has he got any bottles of whisky?
7 Ask "How many?"

Exercise

How much wine *has she got?*
How many cameras *has she got?*

Write four questions:
1 . . . cigarettes . . . ?
2 . . . perfume . . .?
3 . . . watches . . . ?
4 . . . money . . . ?

18 Which one?

George How about some more wine?
Charles Please.
George Which glass is yours?
Charles That one's mine.
George Which one?
Charles The empty one!

George Well, good night . . .
Charles Good night . . . thank you for a lovely evening.
George Now, which coats are yours?
Charles Oh, those coats are ours.
George Which ones?
Charles The black one and the grey one.
George Ah, yes . . . I've got them.
Charles Good. The grey one's mine, and the black one's hers.

Exercise 1

Which one would you like?
I'd like the classical one.

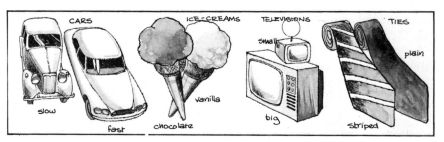

Exercise 2

Which ones would you like?
I'd like the expensive ones.

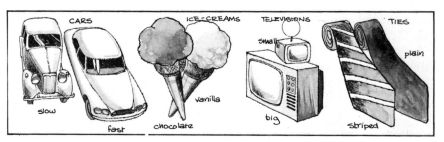

Exercise 3

Which house is theirs?
The big one's theirs.

Which house is his?
The small one's his.

Exercise 4

Example:
It's my pen.   *It's mine.*
They're our books.   *They're ours.*

1 It's his car   · · · ·
2 It's their house   · · · ·
3 It's John's coat   · · · ·
4 It's her hat   · · · ·
5 It's your flat   · · · ·
6 It's Mary's bag   · · · ·

19 Everyday Conversation

O Can you show me some cameras, please?
P Certainly, sir . . . this one's very good.
O Yes, it is . . . . How much is it?
P £85, sir.
O Oh, dear. That's very expensive.
P Hmm, I see . . . that one isn't expensive, sir.
O What make is it?
P It's a Kodak . . . it's £47.
O Hmm . . . Can you show it to me, please?

£85/£92/£78/£63
£47/£39/£26/£51

cameras (Kodak)
radios (Sony)
watches (Timex)
cassette-recorders
  (Philips)

Q Oh, excuse me!
R Yes, sir?
Q Could you bring us some more tea, please?
R Of course, sir.
Q . . . and could you bring me the bill, please? I'm in a hurry.

tea
coffee
cream
brandy

S Taxi!
T Where to, madam?
S Can you take me to the airport, please?
T Certainly, madam. . . . Have you got any luggage?
S Yes. Can you get it for me? It's over there.
T All right. . . . Ooh! It's very heavy.
S Yes, it is . . . I'm very sorry.

airport
station
bus station
International Hotel

U Goodnight, Andrew.
V Goodnight, Colin.
U Have a good holiday!
V Thanks.
U Don't forget . . . send me a postcard!
V O.K. . . . Oh, I haven't got your address.
U That's O.K. You can send it to me at the office.
V All right . . . 'Bye.
U 'Bye.

at the office
at school
at work
here

20 A postcard

Dear John,
This is a picture of Paris. The weather's beautiful. The hotel's excellent. In my hotel room there's a colour T.V. and a shower. The food isn't very good. Paris is expensive. My French is terrible, but the people are friendly. See you soon.
Best wishes, Mary ×××

Mr. John Carter,
13 Nelson Road,
Moss Side,
MANCHESTER,
M17 3JQ
England

Dear Joe,
       Anne,
       Mother,
       Father,

This is a picture of	Cambridge. Bournemouth. London. Oxford.	The weather's	hot. cold. sunny. rainy.	The school is very	good. bad. large. small.

I'm in class	A2. R17. B3. R50.	There are a lot of	Germans Italians Mexicans Brazilians	in my class. My	teacher's name teachers' names	is are	Michael. Pat. David. Sue.

English is very	easy. difficult. interesting.	The town's	boring. exciting. busy. big.	There are a lot of	pubs, discos, theatres, cinemas,	and things are very

cheap. expensive.	The food is	different, terrible, delicious, O.K.	and English people are very	friendly. reserved. warm. cold.	See you	soon. in 3 weeks. in 4 weeks. in 6 weeks.

Best wishes,

21 What are they doing?

Anne Hello, Linda. Is Jack here?
Linda No, he isn't.
Anne Is he working today?
Linda No, he isn't working today. He's in the kitchen.
Anne What's he doing?
Linda He's cooking.
Anne What are you doing?
Linda I'm reading.

Look at the picture.
They're in the night club now.

Exercise 1

He's smoking	. *B* .
He's drinking	. . .
She's singing	. . .
He's sleeping	. . .
They're dancing	. . .
They're eating	. . .

Exercise 2

G *What's he doing? He's writing.*
H . . . .
I . . . .
J . . . .
drawing/typing/reading

Exercise 3

swimming/eating
He's swimming
She isn't swimming
Is she eating? *Yes, she is.*
Is he eating? *No, he isn't.*

reading/writing
. . .
. . .
. . .
. . .

Look at these words:

work	working	smoke	smoking
cook	cooking	dance	dancing
read	reading	write	writing
eat	eating	type	typing
drink	drinking		
sing	singing	sit	sitting
sleep	sleeping	run	running
draw	drawing	swim	swimming

22 Can you help me?

Thomas is a student. He's staying with the Taylors, an English family.

Thomas Hello, Mrs Taylor. Can you help me? I'm doing my homework and I can't understand this word.

Mrs Taylor Which one? Oh . . . that's difficult. I can't help you now . . . I'm watching something . . .

Thomas Oh? What are you watching?

Mrs Taylor I'm watching a cowboy film.

Thomas Can Mr Taylor help me?

Mrs Taylor No, he can't now, Thomas. He's reading.

Thomas What's he reading?

Mrs Taylor He's reading a magazine.

Thomas What about Kate?

Mrs Taylor Oh, she can't help you now . . . she's phoning someone.

Thomas Oh? Who's she phoning?

Mrs Taylor She's phoning her boyfriend . . . you're asking a lot of questions tonight, Thomas!

Thomas Am I? . . . Well, I'm practising my English!

Exercise

Jill and John/tennis.
What are Jill and John *doing?*
They're playing tennis.

Mr Smith/his car
Mary/a letter
Mr and Mrs Jones/television
Bob/a letter
Arthur and Mike/a box
Mrs Brown/the dishes
Tony/beer

drinking
watching
carrying
writing
typing
cleaning
washing

Jill and John

Mary

Mr Smith

Arthur and Mike

Mr & Mrs Jones

Tony

Bob

George is lonely and unhappy.
His friends are busy today.

Mrs Brown

23 Everyday Conversation

A Would you like to come to a party?
B Well, I'd like to . . . but when is it?
A On Saturday evening.
B What a pity! I'm busy on Saturday.
A What are you doing?
B I'm doing my homework.
A Really! . . . Another time perhaps?
B Yes, thanks anyway.

a party
a dance
a picnic
a pop concert
a football match

Saturday
Sunday
Monday
Tuesday
Wednesday
Thursday
Friday

C Excuse me, is this seat free?
D Yes, it is.
C Is it O.K. if I sit here?
D Yes, of course.
C Er, . . . is that your newspaper?
D Yes, it is.
C May I borrow it for a minute, please?
D Yes, certainly.

newspaper
pen
lighter
umbrella
magazine

E Good morning.
F Good morning. Can I help you?
E Yes, I'm looking for a book.
F What's the title?
E *Instant English*. Have you got it?
F Yes, we have.
E How much is it?
F £5.
E May I see it?
F Of course, here you are.

book
 (*Instant English*)
record
 (*Love Story*)
magazine
 (*Today*)
cassette
 (*Instant English*)
dictionary
 (*Oxford English
 Picture Dictionary*)

£5
£1
£4
£7
£3

24 The fashion show

. . . and now here's Julia. Julia's wearing a white cotton blouse, and a black nylon skirt. She's wearing orange shoes, and she's carrying an orange leather handbag.
Thank you, Julia!
　Now, Godfrey's wearing dark-blue flared trousers and a light-blue woollen jacket. He's wearing a yellow terylene shirt and a red tie.
Thank you, Godfrey!

TONY　JUNE

SUNGLASSES

GOLD EAR-RINGS

A SILVER CHAIN

A NECKLACE

A YELLOW T-SHIRT

A GREEN BLOUSE

A DIAMOND RING

A BROWN LEATHER BELT

A PINK TROUSER-SUIT

BLUE JEANS

BLACK SHOES

Exercise
Write sentences about Tony and June.

25 At the cinema

Peter's standing outside the cinema. He's waiting for Lulu, his girlfriend, and he's looking at his watch because she's late. An old man's coming out of the cinema. A young man's going into the cinema. A boy's running up the steps. A woman's buying a ticket from the cashier. Some people are queueing outside the cinema.

Questions

Where's Peter standing?
Who's he waiting for?
What's he looking at?
Why is he looking at his watch?
Who's coming out of the cinema?
Who's going into the cinema?
Who's buying a ticket?
Where are the people queueing?

Now Peter's in the cinema with Lulu. He's sitting between Lulu and a man with a moustache. A lady's sitting in front of him. She's wearing a large hat. Peter can't see the film. A man's sitting behind Peter. He's smoking a pipe. Lulu's unhappy because the smoke's going into her eyes.

Questions

Where's Peter now?
Who's he with?
Where's he sitting?
Who's sitting in front of him?
What's the lady wearing?
Who's sitting behind him?
What's the man smoking?
Why is Lulu unhappy?

This is a scene from the film. In this scene, a beautiful young girl's lying across the lines. She's shouting 'Help!' because the train's coming along the lines. It's very near. It's coming round the bend now.

Questions

Where's the girl lying?
What's she shouting?
Why is she shouting?
Is the train near?
Can you see the train?
Where is it?

26 What's on television tonight?

John Hello, darling. . . . I'm home!

Anne Hello, John. Are you tired, dear?

John Yes, I am. What time is it?

Anne It's six o'clock.

John Oh . . . What's on television tonight?

Anne There's a good programme at quarter past eight . . . 'Paul McCartney In Concert'.

John Yes . . . and there's a good film after the news.

Anne Ooh . . . and 'Mary in Love' at quarter to seven before 'Police Story'.

John Oh, I can't watch that! There's a football match on ITV at half past six.

Anne But, John, it's my favourite programme!

John Well, go and watch it at your mother's!

BBC-1

6.00 The South Today

6.45 Mary in Love (Romantic Comedy)

7.15 Police Story

8.15 In Concert Paul McCartney

9.00 The Nine O'Clock News

9.30 Rock Around The Clock. (Film – 1955)

ITV

6.00 News and Weather

6.30 Football England v. Brazil

8.00 Film: Cleopatra

10.15 Tonight in London

10.45 The Detectives

BBC-2

6.00

7.30

8.00

9.00

International time

1st	2nd	3rd	4th	5th	6th

It's one o'clock in Mexico City   New York   Caracas   Rio de Janeiro   Greenland   The Azores

7th	8th	9th	10th	11th	12th

London   Rome   Istanbul   Baghdad   Abu Dhabi   Karachi

Exercise

What time is it?   . . .   .

It's three o'clock.

27 In prison

Tom Well. . . . Tomorrow we're going to leave this place!

Fred Yes. What are you going to do first?

Tom Hmm . . . first, I'm going to rent a big car, meet my girlfriend and take her to an expensive restaurant. We're going to have steak and drink champagne. What about you, Fred?

Fred My wife's going to meet me outside the prison. Then we're going to have tea with her mother.

Tom With her mother! You're joking!

Fred No, I'm not. I'm going to work for my wife's mother.

Tom Really? You're not going to work for your mother-in-law!

Fred Yes. She's got a little café in London.

Tom What are you going to do there?

Fred I'm going to wash up.

Tom What! Wash up! I'm not going to work! I'm going to have a good time!

Fred You're lucky. . . . I'm going to rob a bank next week.

Tom Why?

Fred Because I'm happy in prison!

Exercise 1

prison
He's going to leave prison.

Write sentences with:
1 car
2 girlfriend
3 good time

Tom

Exercise 2

car
He isn't going to rent a car.

Write sentences with:
1 steak
2 champagne
3 good time

Fred

Exercise 3

steak
They're going to have steak

Write sentences with:
1 car
2 champagne
3 good time

Tom and his girlfriend

Exercise 4

champagne
They aren't going to drink champagne.

Write sentences with:
1 good time
2 steak
3 car

Fred and his wife

28 An English Wedding

1

This is an English wedding. They're standing on the steps outside the church. The bride is wearing a long white dress and is holding some blue flowers in her left hand. The groom is wearing a traditional morning suit and is holding a top hat in his right hand. They're both smiling because they're very happy.

1 What is this?
2 Where are they standing?
3 What's the bride wearing?
4 What's she holding?
5 What's the groom wearing?
6 What's he holding?
7 Why are they smiling?

2

In a few minutes, they're going to get into a Rolls-Royce and drive to a big hotel for the reception. At the reception they're going to cut the cake and drink champagne. Then they're going to open all their presents. Some people are going to make speeches and both of the mothers are going to cry.

1 What are they going to get into?
2 Where are they going to drive?
3 What are they going to cut?
4 What are they going to drink?
5 What are the mothers going to do?

3

At three o'clock they're going to leave the reception and drive to Heathrow Airport. They're going to fly to Bermuda. They're going to spend their honeymoon in a villa by the sea.
They're going to be happy for ever and ever and have a lot of children.

1 What time are they going to leave the reception?
2 Where are they going to drive to?
3 Where are they going to fly to?
4 Where are they going to spend their honeymoon?
5 How many children are they going to have?

29 Computer dating

Interviewer Come in.

Mr Bull Ah, good afternoon. My name's Bull . . . John Bull. I'm looking for a girlfriend.

Interviewer Please sit down, Mr Bull. May I ask you some questions?

Mr Bull Oh, yes . . . what about?

Interviewer Ah . . . music, for example . . . do you like music?

Mr Bull Yes, I do. I like classical music.

Interviewer Do you like pop music?

Mr Bull No, I don't . . . and I don't like jazz.

Interviewer How old are you, Mr Bull?

Mr Bull What! I don't like personal questions!

Interviewer Oh, well . . . can you complete this form later, and send it by post!

Exercise 1

Look at John Bull:
Does he like beer?
Write 5 questions.

Exercise 2

Do you like football?
Write 5 questions.

Exercise 3

Look at Virginia Cherry:
1 *She likes dancing.*
2 *She doesn't like television.*
Write ten sentences.

Exercise 4

1 *I like films.*
2 *I don't like dogs.*
Write 10 sentences.

Passport photograph

Surname:	Bull
First Name(s):	John George
Age:	65
Occupation:	Farmer

Likes:
Colours: Red, white and blue.
Food: Roast beef, potatoes
Drink: Beer, whiskey
Recreation: Fishing, chess, golf
Music: Classical music

Dislikes: Pop music, Dancing Films, children.
Date: 29.6.78
Signature: John Bull.

Passport photograph

Surname:	CHERRY
First Name(s):	VIRGINIA
Age:	18
Occupation:	STUDENT

Likes:
Colours: PINK, YELLOW AND GREEN
Food: FRUIT, VEGETABLES
Drink: MILK, FRUIT JUICE
Recreation: DANCING, SWIMMING, TENNIS
Music: ROCK, JAZZ

Dislikes: POLITICS, TELEVISION, FOOTBALL, DOGS, BEARDS
Date: 29TH JUNE 1978
Signature: Virginia Cherry

30 I want you, Fiona

Charles Please marry me, Fiona. I want you, I need you, I love you.

Fiona I'm sorry Charles, but I can't.

Charles Oh, Fiona. Why not?

Fiona Well, Charles. I like you . . . I like you a lot . . . but I don't love you.

Charles But Fiona, love isn't everything.

Fiona Oh, Charles, you don't understand . . . for me love is everything.

Charles Do you love another man Fiona?

Fiona Yes Charles, I do . . . James.

Charles Not James Milton!

Fiona Yes, James Milton.

Charles But he doesn't want you. He's engaged.

Fiona I know.

Charles But Fiona, James isn't a rich man. I can give you everything. What do you want? Clothes? Money? Travel? A big house?

Fiona No, Charles. I don't want those things. I only want James.

Questions

Who wants Fiona?
Does he love her?
Does Fiona like Charles?
Does she like him a lot?
Does she love him?
Does Fiona love another man?
What's his name?
Does James want Fiona?
Is he rich?
Is Charles rich?
What can he give Fiona?
Does she want clothes?
Does she want money?
What does she want?

Exercise 1

Who wants Fiona?
Charles wants Fiona.

Who loves Fiona?
Who needs Fiona?
Who wants James?
Who loves James?

Exercise 2

Who does Charles want?
Charles wants Fiona.

Who does Charles love?
Who does Fiona love?
Who does Fiona want?
Who does Charles need?

31 Everyday Conversation

G What are you doing this weekend?
H I'm going away.
G Oh, where are you going?
H I'm going to London.
G How long for?
H Just for two days.

this weekend
on Saturday
on Friday
tomorrow
next week

London
Wales
Scotland
Ireland
Paris

I Have you got a car?
J Yes, I have.
I What kind is it?
J It's a V.W.
I Do you like it?
J Yes, I do.
I Why?
J Because it's very economical.

V.W.
Ford
Datsun
Fiat
Jaguar

economical
big
comfortable
modern
fast

K Excuse me . . .
L Yes?
K Have you got any change?
L What do you need?
K I need some tens.
L Oh, how many do you want?
K Well, can you change a pound note?
L Yes, I think so.

Coins: 1p, 2p, 5p, 10p, 50p
Notes: £1, £5, £10, £20
a pound note
a five-pound note
a ten-pound note
a twenty-pound note

M Good afternoon.
N Good afternoon.
M Could you repair these shoes, please?
N Yes, certainly. When do you want them?
M As soon as possible.
N Is Thursday afternoon O.K?
M Yes, that's fine.

these shoes
these glasses
these boots
this camera
this watch
this radio

Thursday afternoon
Tuesday evening
Wednesday morning

32 An interview

Robin Knight, the television reporter, is interviewing the Duchess of Wessex for the programme 'The English At Home'.

Robin Now, Duchess . . . tell us about an ordinary day in your life.

Duchess Well, I wake up at seven o'clock . . .

Robin Really? Do you get up then?

Duchess No, of course I don't get up at that time. I have breakfast in bed and I read 'The Times'.

Robin What time do you get up?

Duchess I get up at ten.

Robin What do you do then?

Duchess I read my letters and dictate the replies to my secretary.

Robin . . . and then?

Duchess At eleven I walk in the garden with Philip.

Robin Oh? Who's Philip?

Duchess Philip's my dog.

Robin What time do you have lunch?

Duchess I have lunch at twelve thirty.

Robin And after lunch?

Duchess Oh, I rest until six o'clock.

Robin . . . and at six? What do you do at six?

Duchess I dress for dinner. We have dinner at eight o'clock.

Robin What time do you go to bed?

Duchess Well, I have a bath at nine thirty, and I go to bed at ten.

Robin Thank you, Duchess . . . you certainly have a busy and interesting life!

Questions

Who's interviewing the Duchess of Wessex?
Does she wake up at eight o'clock?
Ask "What time?"
Does she have breakfast in the kitchen?
Ask "Where?"
Does she read 'Time' Magazine?
Ask "What?"
Does she read her letters?
Does she dictate the replies to her husband?

Does she walk in the garden with her secretary?
Ask "Who with?"
Does she have lunch at twelve?
Ask "What time?"
What does she do until six?
What does she do at six?
Does she have dinner at seven?
Ask "What time?"
Does she go to bed at nine thirty?
Ask "What time?"

Exercise

A *She reads* 'The Times'.
B *She doesn't read* 'Time' magazine.
C *Does she read* 'The Sun'?

A She walks with her dog.
B . . . with her secretary.
C . . . with her husband?

A She dresses for dinner.
B . . . breakfast.
C . . . lunch?

33 Every day

1 Alan's a lorry driver.
2 He's twenty-five years old.
3 He works five days a week.
4 He gets up at six o'clock every day.
5 He eats an enormous breakfast.
6 He drinks two cups of tea.
7 Then he kisses his wife.
8 He leaves for work at half past six.
9 He has lunch in a transport café.
10 He comes home at five o'clock.
11 In the evening he goes to the pub.
12 He goes to bed at ten o'clock.

Questions

1 What does Alan do?
2 How old is Alan?
3 How many days a week does he work?
4 What time does he get up?
5 What does he eat for breakfast?
6 What does he drink?
7 What does he do after breakfast?
8 What time does he leave for work?
9 Where does he have lunch?
10 What time does he come home?
11 Where does he go in the evening?
12 What time does he go to bed?

Exercise 1

Now ask (and answer) questions about these people:

Judith

Peter and Paul

Cecil

Judith	Peter and Paul	Cecil
1 secretary	1 schoolboys	1 playboy
2 18	2 12	2 42
3 the office/5 days a week	3 school/5 days a week	3 not/work/5 days a week
4 7.30	4 eight o'clock	4 eleven o'clock
5 nothing	5 cornflakes	5 caviare
6 orange-juice	6 milk	6 vodka
7 parents	7 mother	7 fifth wife
8 the office/8.15	8 school/8.45	8 the pub/twelve o'clock
9 in the canteen	9 at school	9 in a pub
10 home/5.30	10 home/four o'clock	10 not/come home
11 evening classes	11 television	11 casino
12 eleven o'clock	12 nine o'clock	12 five o'clock in the morning

Exercise 2

Write twelve sentences about Cecil.

34 What's My Job?

Chairman Good evening, Ladies and Gentlemen. Welcome to *What's My Job?* Here's our first competitor. We've got three famous people here — Professor Moore, the scientist — Jessica Gale, the film star — and Ken Carson, the pop singer. They're going to ask the questions. First, Professor Moore . . .

Professor Hmm. . . . Do you work outside?

Competitor No, I don't.

Professor Do you wear a uniform?

Competitor No, I don't.

Professor I see. Do you work in an office?

Competitor No, I don't.

Chairman Next . . . Jessica Gale.

Jessica Oh . . . Is your job important?

Competitor Yes, it is.

Jessica Do you get a big salary?

Competitor Yes, I do.

Jessica Have you got any special diplomas?

Competitor Yes, I have.

Chairman Thank you, Jessica . . . and now Ken Carson.

Ken Hello. Do you work with your hands?

Competitor Yes, I do.

Ken Do you work at weekends?

Competitor No, I don't.

Ken Do you travel?

Competitor No, I don't.

Chairman That's the ninth question! Now you can ask one last question.

Jessica Ha . . . Are you a doctor?

Competitor No, I'm not . . . I'm a dentist.

Electrician   Teacher   Artist   Secretary   Ballet dancer   Bank manager

35 Never on a Sunday

Vicar Ah, good evening, Mr Benson. I never see you in church nowadays.

Benson Oh! No, Vicar . . . but my wife always goes to church . . . she goes every Sunday.

Vicar I know . . . but you never come.

Benson Well, I sometimes come, Vicar. I come on Christmas Day and at Easter.

Vicar Hmm . . . But what about Sundays, Mr Benson?

Benson I usually wash my car on Sunday morning.

Vicar I see. Why don't you wash your car on Saturday next week, Mr Benson?

Benson Oh . . . I can't do that, Vicar.

Vicar Why not?

Benson It's my son's wedding next Saturday . . . I'm going to church!

Exercise 1

He/sometimes/football.
He sometimes *plays* football.

1 They/often/potatoes.
2 She/usually/a skirt.
3 I/never/a hat.
4 He/occasionally/radio.
5 We/rarely/vodka.
6 You/never/cigarettes.

Exercise 2

coffee
I sometimes drink coffee
or
I never drink coffee
or
I often drink coffee

Now, write true sentences:

1 coffee	**7** a newspaper
2 television	**8** cinema
3 golf	**9** new clothes
4 spaghetti	**10** a tie
5 wine	**11** cigarettes
6 caviare	**12** pop music

1 Every morning he cleans his teeth. He *always* cleans his teeth in the morning.

2 She gets up at 7 o'clock from Monday to Saturday, but on Sunday she gets up at 11 o'clock. She *usually* gets up at 7 o'clock.

3 They like films. They see all the new films. They *often* go to the cinema.

4 He's got a radio and a television. He *sometimes* listens to the radio, and he *sometimes* watches television.

5 Her brother lives in London. She doesn't. She sees him four or five times every year. She *occasionally* sees him.

6 He doesn't usually smoke, but at Christmas, after dinner, he has a cigar. He *rarely* smokes cigars.

7 She doesn't like whisky. She *never* drinks whisky.

36 A Questionnaire

Desmond Philton works for a Market Research company. He's asking people about their free time.

Desmond Good evening, sir.

Mr Norris Good evening.

Desmond I'm from Market Research Ltd. May I ask you some questions?

Mr Norris Yes, . . . yes, all right.

Desmond Thank you. . . . Now, what time do you usually arrive home from work?

Mr Norris Hmm . . . I usually arrive home at six o'clock.

Desmond When do you usually have dinner?

Mr Norris Oh, I usually eat at seven o'clock, but I sometimes eat at eight o'clock or nine o'clock. My wife works too!

Desmond What do you usually do after dinner?

Mr Norris Well, I sometimes go out, but I usually stay at home and watch television.

Desmond How often do you go out?

Mr Norris Oh, not often . . . once or twice a week.

Desmond Do you often visit your friends?

Mr Norris Yes, I do, quite often. I sometimes visit them, and they sometimes visit me.

Desmond Do you ever go to the cinema?

Mr Norris Oh, yes . . . yes, I do.

Desmond How often?

Mr Norris Well, I occasionally see a film . . . I like horror films . . . *Frankenstein* or *Dracula!*

Desmond . . . and the theatre? Do you ever go to the theatre?

Mr Norris Yes, I do . . . but not often. I rarely go to the theatre.

Desmond Hmm . . . Do you ever go to the ballet?

Mr Norris No, never. I don't like ballet.

Desmond Well, thank you Mr Norris . . .

Mr Norris May I ask you a question?

Desmond Yes?

Mr Norris What do you do in your free time?

Desmond I ask questions, Mr Norris. . . . I never answer them.

Mr Norris Oh!

MARKET RESEARCH LTD

QUESTIONNAIRE

1. What time do you usually arrive home?

before six o'clock	
at six o'clock	
after six o'clock	

2. What do you usually do after dinner?

watch television	
read	
go out	
visit friends	

3. How often do you (a) go out? (b) watch television? (c) visit friends?

	(a)	(b)	(c)
rarely			
once or twice a week			
three or four times a week			
every night			

4. Do you ever go to

	never	rarely	occasionally	sometimes	often
the cinema?					
the ballet?					
the theatre?					
the opera?					

37 What does he do every day?

Hello! My name's Douglas Hunter. I'm a pilot for British Airways. I fly Concordes. I'm not working today. I'm playing golf. It's my favourite sport.

Questions

What's his name?
What's his job?
What does he do?
What's he doing now?
What's his favourite sport?

This man is a champion jockey. His name's Gordon Lester. He rides racehorses, but he isn't riding a racehorse at the moment. He's dancing with his sixth wife.

Questions

What's his name?
What's his job?
Is he a good jockey?
Where is he now?
What's he doing?
Who's he with?

This is a picture of Bob and Michael. They teach English in a language school. They aren't teaching at the moment. They're in the pub. They're talking and laughing about their students.

Questions

Who are they?
Do they teach?
What do they teach?
Where are they now?
What are they doing?

This is Rosalind Graham. She dances for the Royal Ballet. She isn't dancing now. She's having a bath. She's going to dance in front of the Queen this evening.

Questions

What's her name?
What does she do?
Is she dancing now?
What is she doing?
What is she going to do?

Exercise

Kevin Shannon, footballer.

Example:
a *What does he do? He plays football.*

b *What's he doing? He's sleeping.*

Kathleen and Kate, singers.

a . . . .
  . . . .
b . . . .
  . . . .

Lucy, typist.

a . . . .
  . . . .
b . . . .
  . . . .

38 Well or badly?

There's an international football match on television. England are playing against Scotland. They are good teams. They usually play well. But today England are playing very well, and Scotland are playing badly.

Questions

What's on television?
Which teams are playing?
Are they good teams?
Do they usually play well or badly?
How are England playing today?
How are Scotland playing today?

Tom Morgan often has accidents. This is his fourth accident this year. He's a bad driver, because he's a fast and careless driver. He drives fast, carelessly and badly.

Questions

What's his name?
Does he often have accidents?
Is this his first accident this year?
Is he a good or a bad driver?
Does he drive well or badly?
Is he a fast or a slow driver?
Does he drive carefully or carelessly?

Bill Morris is a gentleman. He always drives slowly, carefully and well. All his friends say, 'Bill's a good driver! He's very careful.'

Questions

What's his name?
Is he a gentleman?
Is he a good driver or a bad driver?
Does he drive well or badly?
Is he a fast driver or a slow driver?
Does he drive carefully or does he drive carelessly?

Mr Johnson works very hard. He's a fast worker. His boss often says, 'Johnson works fast for 10 hours every day. He's a very hard worker.'

Questions

What's his name?
Is he a hard worker or a lazy worker?
Does he work hard or lazily?
Is he a fast or a slow worker?
Does he work fast or slowly?

Exercise

Kevin's a good player.
How does he play?
He plays well.

1 You're a bad swimmer.
2 She's a careful driver.
3 John's a slow learner.
4 They're hard workers.
5 He's a fast walker.

Look at this:

bad	badly	happy	happily	good	well
slow	slowly	busy	busily	fast	fast
careful	carefully	noisy	noisily	hard	hard
careless	carelessly				

39 Everyday Conversation

O How do you come to school?
P By bus.
O How much does it cost?
P Only 20p.
O How long does it take?
P About twenty minutes.

bus
train
tube
taxi

twenty minutes
an hour
half an hour
quarter of an hour

Q Is Maria Italian?
R Yes, I think so.
Q Does she speak English well?
R No, I don't think so.
Q Is she coming to the dance tonight?
R I hope so!

Italian
Portuguese
Venezuelan
Mexican
Iranian

dance
party
discotheque
pub
club

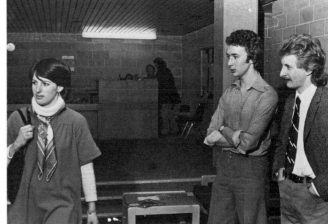

S What's the matter?
T I've got a cold.
S Why don't you see a doctor?
T I don't know any doctors.
S Why don't you ask your landlady?
T Yes. That's a good idea.

a cold
a sore throat
stomach-ache
back-ache
a temperature

your landlady
your teacher
the principal
your friends

U Would you like to dance?
V Yes.
U Do you come here often?
V Sometimes.
U Do you live here?
V Yes, I do.
U Where do you work?
V In a bank.
U Do you like it?
V It's O.K.

sometimes
once a week
twice a week
every night
occasionally

a bank
an office
a factory
a shop
a hospital

40 A personal letter

13 rue Pigalle,
Montmartre,
Paris.
August 9th, 1977

Dear John,

Well, this is my second week in Paris. I like it very much. I usually get up at ten o'clock and have breakfast in a street café. French breakfasts are very small, but the coffee's not bad. I always go to school by Metro. I usually arrive at school at twelve o'clock. I'm learning a lot of French. School usually finishes at five o'clock. In the evening I occasionally stay in the hotel, but I usually go out for dinner with a friend. Life is very interesting here. Next weekend I'm going to the coast. Give my regards to everybody.

Love, Mary xxx

Carter,
on Road,
Side,
NCHESTER
7 3JQ
ngland

Dear	Joe,								
	Anne,								
	Mother,								
	Father,								

Well, this is my	second	week	on holiday.	I	like it	very much.	I	usually	get up at
	third		in England.		don't like it			always	
	fourth		here.						

	seven o'clock,	and have breakfast	with my landlady.	English breakfasts are very	big.
	7.30,		in a restaurant.		small.
	eight o'clock,		in the hotel.		good.

I	sometimes	go to school	on foot.	I usually arrive at school at	nine o'clock.	In the evenings
	usually		by bus.		eleven o'clock.	
	always		by car.		one o'clock.	

I	usually	stay at home, but	sometimes	I go out to	the cinema	and	see a film.
	sometimes		usually		a discotheque		dance.
	occasionally		occasionally		a restaurant		talk to my friends.

Life is very	busy	here.	Tomorrow	I'm going	to a pub.	Give my	best wishes	to
	boring		Next week		on an excursion.		regards	
	quiet		On Sunday		to the cinema.		love	

	your parents.
	Tom.
	the family.

Love,

41 Where were you yesterday?

Detective Now, Mr Briggs . . . where were you yesterday?

Briggs Yesterday? What time?

Detective At two o'clock. Where were you at two o'clock?

Briggs I was at home.

Detective You weren't at home, you were in central London.

Briggs No, I wasn't! I was at home! Ask my girlfriend! She was with me!

Detective Well, we're going to speak to her later. Where is she now?

Briggs Oh . . . I don't know . . .

Detective O.K. . . . now, where were you on January 12th?

Briggs January 12th?

Detective Yes, it was a Wednesday.

Briggs I can't remember.

Detective You were in Manchester.

Briggs Oh no, I wasn't.

Detective Oh yes, you were.

Briggs Oh no, I wasn't . . . I was in prison in January.

Detective Oh!

Questions

Where were you at one o'clock?	I was at home.
five past two?	school.
ten past three?	work.
quarter past four?	the pub.
half past five?	the cinema.
twenty-five to six?	the supermarket.
twenty to seven?	
quarter to eight?	

Questions

When were you in England?	I was there in January.
Europe?	February.
Mexico?	March.
London?	April.
Spain?	May.
Holland?	June.
Italy?	July.
	August.
	September.
	October.
	November.
	December.

Exercise 1

Look at this example:
I/here/two o'clock
I was here at two o'clock.

1 He/Italy/July
2 They/home/Sunday
3 You/here/one o'clock
4 She/school/yesterday
5 It/cold/January
6 We/London/Wednesday

Exercise 2

Look at this example:
You/New York/February?
Were you in New York in February?

1 she/home/Thursday?
2 it/hot/June?
3 they/at work/five-thirty?
4 he/England/November?
5 you/there/four o'clock?
6 they/Russia/December?

42 Holidays

Donald Hello, John! Where were you last month?

John Oh, I was on holiday.

Donald Oh, really? . . . but you were on holiday in January.

John Yes, I was in Switzerland in January.

Donald Where were you last month?

John I was in Florida.

Donald Florida! What was it like?

John Fantastic! The weather was beautiful . . . the sea was warm.

Donald What was the hotel like?

John Excellent! There was a swimming-pool and private beach. There were three restaurants and two bars.

Donald What were the people like?

John They were very friendly.

Donald Was your wife with you?

John No, she wasn't. She never comes with me on holiday.

Donald What about the children? Were they with you?

John No, they weren't. They were with their grandparents.

HOTEL ROYAL ★★★
☆ A SWIMMING POOL!
☆ THREE RESTAURANTS!
☆ A PRIVATE BEACH!
☆ TWO BARS!
☆ A DISCOTHEQUE!
☆ TWO ORCHESTRAS!
☆ A CASINO!
☆ FOUR TENNIS COURTS!

Exercise 1

There was a swimming pool.
There were three restaurants.
Now you write sentences.

Exercise 2

weather
What was the weather *like?*

restaurants
What were the restaurants *like?*

1 service	4 beaches
2 shops	5 hotel
3 food	6 people

43 Everyday Conversation

W Can you change this pullover, please?
X Why? What's wrong with it?
W It's the wrong size.
X Is it too big, or too small?
W It's too small for me.
X What size are you?
W I'm not sure. Can you measure me?
X Yes, certainly. . . . You're a thirty-six. This one's the right size.

pullover
cardigan
nightdress
T-shirt
blouse

Y I'd like a room, please.
Z A single room or a double room sir?
Y A double, please.
Z With or without a private bathroom?
Y With, please.
Z For how many nights?
Y Just for one night, please.

a private bathroom
a shower
a balcony
a colour television

A Excuse me!
B Yes?
A I think my change is wrong!
B Are you sure? Let me see. Oh, yes . . . you need another 50p.
A Yes, that's right.
B I'm terribly sorry.
A That's O.K.

50p
21p
32p
43p
54p

C I think English food is excellent.
D Really! I don't think so.
C Why not?
D I prefer French food.

food
coffee
beer
butter
cheese

French
Turkish
German
Danish
Swiss

44 Return from Space

Phil Strongarm, the American astronaut, is talking to a reporter about his journey to the moon.

Reporter Well, Phil . . . Welcome home!

Phil Thank you.

Reporter Did you have any problems on the journey?

Phil Well, we didn't have any serious problems . . . but it certainly wasn't a holiday!

Reporter Of course not . . .

Phil We didn't have a wash or a shave for two weeks!

Reporter Really?

Phil Yes. It wasn't very comfortable!

Reporter What about food? Was that a problem?

Phil Well, we didn't have any normal food.

Reporter What did you have?

Phil Well, we had some food tablets.

Reporter Are you going to the moon again?

Phil I hope so. It was wonderful!

Questions

Who's Phil Strongarm?
Who's he talking to?
What's he talking about?
Is he English or American?
Did he have any problems on the journey?
Were they serious problems?
Did they have a wash?
Did they have a shave?
Were they comfortable or uncomfortable?
Did they have any normal food?
What did they have?
Is Phil going to the moon again?

Exercise 1

I/breakfast/eight o'clock.
I had breakfast at eight o'clock.

1 You/coffee/eleven o'clock
2 He/lunch/12.30
3 She/tea/3.30
4 They/dinner/eight o'clock
5 We/supper/nine o'clock

Exercise 2

they/a holiday/last year?
Did they have a holiday last year?

1 he/a haircut/last week?
2 you/a good time/last night?
3 she/a birthday/last month?
4 they/a party/last weekend?
5 you/a swim/last Saturday?

Exercise 3

We/a lesson/Sunday
We didn't have a lesson on Sunday.

1 He/a shave/Saturday
2 She/a shower/Monday
3 We/a drink/Tuesday
4 I/a bath/Thursday
5 He/a lecture/Friday

45 Yes, dear!

Every Saturday Mr Brown goes to town. He went to town last Saturday. He usually has a drink in the pub with his friends. Last Saturday he had four or five drinks. After the pub, he usually goes to the supermarket and gets the food for his wife. He got the food last Saturday. He usually comes home on foot. Last Saturday he came home by taxi. His wife was very angry.

Questions

Does he usually go to town on Saturday?
What about last Saturday?
Does he usually have a drink?
What about last Saturday?
Does he usually get the food?
What about last Saturday?
Does he usually come home on foot?
What about last Saturday?

Mrs Brown John! Is that you?
Mr Brown Yes, dear. I'm back.
Mrs Brown Did you come home by taxi?
Mr Brown Yes, dear. The bags were very heavy.
Mrs Brown Did you get everything?
Mr Brown Yes, dear. I got everything . . . nearly everything.
Mrs Brown Nearly everything?
Mr Brown Yes, dear . . . I went to the butcher's, but they didn't have any steak.
Mrs Brown They didn't have any steak!
Mr Brown No, dear, so I got some hamburgers.
Mrs Brown Did you go to the baker's?
Mr Brown Yes, dear . . . but I didn't get any bread.
Mrs Brown You didn't get any bread!
Mr Brown No, dear. They didn't have any bread, so I got some rolls.
Mrs Brown How many rolls did you get?
Mr Brown I can't remember, dear.
Mrs Brown John?
Mr Brown Yes, dear?
Mrs Brown Did you go to the pub again?
Mr Brown Yes, dear.
Mrs Brown How many drinks did you have?
Mr Brown Only four or five, dear, . . . small ones.

Exercise

They had some hamburgers.
They didn't have any steak.
Did they have any chicken?
1 He came home by taxi.
 . . . on foot.
 . . . by bus?
2 He went to the butcher's
 . . . chemist's.
 . . . baker's?
3 He got some rolls.
 . . . bread.
 . . . hamburgers?

46 In the office

Secretary Good afternoon, Mr Smith.

Mr Smith Good afternoon, Miss Wild. Did you finish those letters?

Secretary Yes, sir. I typed them and signed them for you.

Mr Smith Did you photo-copy them?

Secretary Yes, sir. I photo-copied them and posted them.

Mr Smith Did Mr Jackson arrive?

Secretary Yes, sir.

Mr Smith What time did he arrive?

Secretary About two o'clock, sir . . . but he didn't stay. He didn't have time.

Mr Smith What did he want?

Secretary Oh . . . I didn't ask, sir.

Mr Smith Er . . . Did you telephone Mrs Smith?

Secretary Yes, I did . . . but she wasn't in.

Mr Smith Hmm . . . And the table at "Mario's" for tonight?

Secretary Yes, sir, I reserved a table for two, at eight o'clock.

Mr Smith Good! Did Lulu telephone?

Secretary Yes, sir.

Exercise

Who typed the letters?
Miss Wild *typed the letters.*
Mr Smith *didn't type the letters.*
Did Lulu *type the letters?*

1 Who signed the letters?
Miss Wild . . . .
Mr Smith . . . .
. . . Lulu . . . ?

2 Who posted the letters?
Miss Wild . . . .
Mr Smith . . . .
. . . Lulu . . . ?

3 Who photo-copied the letters?
Miss Wild . . . .
Mr Smith . . . .
. . . Lulu . . . ?

47 The Story of Willy The Kid

WILLY THE KID ARRIVED IN DODGE CITY ONE EVENING.

HE WALKED INTO THE SALOON, AND LOOKED SLOWLY ROUND THE ROOM.

EVERYBODY WAS AFRAID. WILLY HAD TWO GUNS.

THE SHERIFF WAS IN HIS OFFICE. HE WAS ASLEEP.

THE SALOON BARMAN RUSHED INTO THE SHERIFF'S OFFICE.

THE SHERIFF HURRIED TO THE SALOON.

THE SHERIFF SHOUTED TO WILLY.

WILLY REPLIED CALMLY.

THEY WALKED INTO THE STREET. THE SHERIFF WAITED. WILLY MOVED HIS HAND TOWARDS HIS GUN...

THE SHERIFF PULLED OUT HIS GUN. HE FIRED TWICE.

THE FIRST BULLET MISSED WILLY. THE SECOND KILLED HIM.

TWO COWBOYS CARRIED WILLY AWAY. THAT WAS THE END OF WILLY THE KID.

Exercise 1

1 He walked into the saloon.
2 He didn't . . . into the Sheriff's office.
3 Did he . . . into the bank?

Exercise 2

1 They carried Willy away.
2 They . . . carry the Sheriff away.
3 . . . they . . . the barman away?

48 Foreign holidays

Anne's a student at London University. She studies Spanish, and she goes to Spain every summer. She lies in the sun, she drinks a lot of wine, and eats a lot of Spanish food. She always flies by British Airways.

Questions

1 Is Anne a student?
2 Does she study French?
3 Ask "What?"
4 Does she go to France every summer?
5 Ask "Where?"
6 What does she do in Spain?
7 How does she travel to Spain?

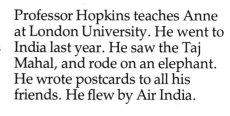

Professor Hopkins teaches Anne at London University. He went to India last year. He saw the Taj Mahal, and rode on an elephant. He wrote postcards to all his friends. He flew by Air India.

Questions

1 Who does he teach?
2 Where did he go last year?
3 What did he see?
4 What did he ride on?
5 Who did he write to?
6 Did he fly by Air India or T.W.A.?

Her mother and father went to Italy last year. They toured Italy by coach. They saw a lot of interesting places. They ate spaghetti in Rome, drank coffee in Venice, and took a lot of photographs. The sun shone every day. They went to Italy by coach.

Questions

1 Where did they go?
2 How did they tour Italy?
3 What did they eat?
4 What did they drink?
5 How many photographs did they take?
6 What was the weather like?
7 Did they go to Italy by coach or by train?

Rob is Anne's boyfriend. He hitch-hiked around the United States last summer. He stayed there for a month. Of course he ate hamburgers, and drank Coca-Cola! He met a lot of interesting people. He bought a lot of American pop records, and brought them back to England. He flew there by Pan-American.

Questions

1 Where did Rob go last summer?
2 How long did he stay?
3 What did he eat?
4 What did he drink?
5 Who did he meet?
6 What did he buy?
7 What did he bring back?
8 Did he fly by Pan-American or T.W.A.?

Exercise

a Anne/go/Spain
b He/not/Spain
c you/Spain?

a Anne *went to* Spain.
b He *didn't go to* Spain.
c *Did* you *go to* Spain?

a They/eat/spaghetti
b He/not/spaghetti
c you/spaghetti?

a They/drink/coffee
b She/not/coffee
c you/coffee?

a He/see/Taj Mahal
b She/not/TajMahal
c you/Taj Mahal?

a He/buy/records
b They/not/records
c you/records?

Look at this

have	had
come	came
go	went
get	got
see	saw
eat	ate
drink	drank
take	took
fly	flew
shine	shone
meet	met
write	wrote
ride	rode
buy	bought
bring	brought

49 Survivors

Bill Craig and John Fitzgerald are pilots. Last year their plane crashed in the Pacific Ocean. They were in a rubber dinghy for four weeks.

They didn't have much water, and they didn't have many things to eat.

They had a few bananas and a little brandy from their plane. They caught a lot of fish.

They had only a little chocolate. They had only a few biscuits and a few apples.

After four weeks, they saw a ship and the ship rescued them.

Questions

What are their names?
What do they do?
Did their plane crash?
Ask "When?"
Ask "Where?"
How many weeks were they in a dinghy?
How much water did they have?
Did they have many bananas?
Did they have much brandy?

Did they catch any fish?
Ask "How many?"
How much chocolate did they have?
How many biscuits did they have?
How many apples did they have?
What did they see after four weeks?

Exercise 1

chocolate

A Did they have any chocolate?
B Yes, they did, but they didn't have much.

A How much chocolate did they have?
B They had only a little.

water

petrol

brandy

Exercise 2

matches

A Did they have any matches?
B Yes, they did, but they didn't have many.

A How many matches did they have?
B They had only a few.

biscuits

apples

bananas

Exercise 3

He hasn't got *much* money.
He's got only *a little* money.

She hasn't got *many* dollars.
She's got only *a few* dollars.

1 He hasn't got . . . friends
2 He's got only . . . friends
3 He hasn't got . . . wine
4 He's got only . . . wine

5 She didn't have . . . Swiss francs
6 She had only . . . French francs
7 There isn't . . . petrol
8 We've got only . . . petrol

50 Robbie and the Rebels

Jill Good morning, Shirley . . .

Shirley Hello, Jill . . .

Jill Oh, I'm tired this morning!

Shirley Are you? Why?

Jill Well, I went to the concert last night.

Shirley Which concert?

Jill The pop concert, the one at the Town Hall.

Shirley Oh, which group did you see?

Jill I saw 'Robbie and the Rebels' . . . they're a new group.

Shirley Are they good?

Jill Hmm . . . they usually play well, but last night they played badly.

Shirley Is Robbie a good singer?

Jill Oh, yes, he usually sings well.

Shirley Did he sing well last night?

Jill No, he didn't . . . he sang very badly.

Shirley What about the group?

Jill Oh, the guitarist played beautifully . . . but the drummer was loud.

Shirley Yes, pop drummers always play loudly.

Jill I know! I had a headache after the concert.

Shirley Hmm . . . I never go to pop concerts. I prefer classical music.

Questions

What are their names?
Who's tired?
Ask "Why?"
Which concert did she go to?
Which group did she see?
How do they usually play?
How did they play last night?
How does Robbie usually sing?
How did he sing last night?
How did the guitarist play?
Do pop drummers always play loudly?
Did Jill have a headache before the concert?
Ask "When?"
Does Shirley prefer pop music or classical music?

Exercise 1

He's a good singer.
He usually sings well.

1 They're beautiful dancers
2 She's a careless writer.
3 He's a hard worker.
4 He's a bad player.
5 They're good drivers.

Exercise 2

He usually sings well, *but yesterday he sang badly.*

1 She usually writes carefully, ...
2 She usually types slowly, ...
3 They usually play badly, ...
4 He usually works fast, ...
5 He usually answers carelessly, ...

51 Everyday Conversation

E Excuse me . . . I lost my handbag this morning.
F Where did you lose it?
E On the bus . . . I left it on the number 28.
F Well, you're lucky, the conductor found it.
E Thank goodness! I was worried.
F Here it is . . . he gave it to me an hour ago.

handbag
camera
wallet
purse
umbrella

an hour ago
two hours ago
three hours ago
half an hour ago
25 minutes ago

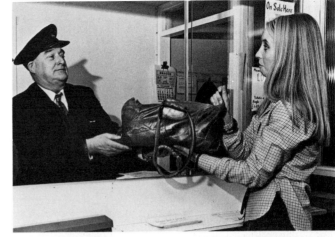

G What did you do last weekend?
H I went to Oxford.
G Really? How did you go?
H I went by car.
G How long did it take?
H It took about two hours.

last weekend
last Saturday
last Monday
last Friday

by car
by train
by bus
by taxi

I Hello, John! I thought you were in Brighton!
J I was. I drove there on Friday.
I Yes . . . ?
J . . . and I came back on Saturday morning!
I Oh? Why did you come back?
J Well, I went to a casino, and spent all my money!
I How did you do that?
J Well, I won a little at first . . . then I lost everything!

Brighton
Bournemouth
London
Torquay

Saturday morning
Sunday evening
Monday evening
Tuesday afternoon
this morning

K Have a cigarette.
L No, thanks. I'm trying to stop.
K Oh, come on! I insist!
L No, really . . . I've got a terrible cough.

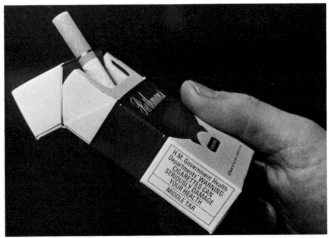

52 The Eight O'Clock News

Good evening. And here is the
Eight O'Clock News.

Last night there was a revolution
in Mandanga. The rebels attacked
the President's palace, shot the
President and burnt the building.
The air force bombed the capital.
The United States sent ships to the
area this morning. The Soviet
Union protested in the United
Nations.

Questions

What happened in Mandanga?
Ask "When?"
What did the rebels attack?
Did they shoot the Prime Minister?
Ask "Who?"
What did they burn?
Did they bomb the capital?
What did the United States do?
What did the Soviet Union do?

The Scottish police are looking for
two climbers in the Highlands.
The climbers left yesterday
morning to climb Ben Nevis. It
began to snow heavily yesterday
afternoon. The police sent out a
search party yesterday evening.
They spent the night on the
mountain, but they didn't find the
climbers.

Questions

How many climbers are the police
 looking for?
Ask "Where?"
When did they leave?
What did they want to climb?
Did it rain or did it snow?
Who sent out a search party?
Ask "When?"
Did they spend the night in a hotel?
Ask "Where?"
Did they find the climbers?

The Queen opened a new hospital
in London today. She met all the
doctors and nurses, and spoke to
the first patients. The Queen wore
a yellow dress, and a green hat.

Questions

Who opened a hospital?
Ask "Where?"
Ask "When?"
Who did the Queen meet?
Who did the Queen speak to?
What did she wear?

. . . and next football. This
afternoon at Wembley Stadium,
England played against Wales.
England lost by four goals to nil.
The English captain broke his leg.
The Welsh team played well.
David Evans scored three goals for
Wales.

Questions

Who did England play against?
Ask "Where?"
Did they win or did they lose?
Which team played well?
Ask "How many goals?"
Who broke his leg?
Who scored three goals?

53 Howard Hughes 1905-1976
Biography of a Billionaire

24th December 1905 Howard Hughes was born in Houston, Texas.

1912 He started school.

1924 His father died. He left school. He inherited $750,000. He became director of his father's oil-drilling company.

1925 He married Ella Rice.

1927 He went to Hollywood.

1928 He produced a film. He divorced Ella Rice.

1930 He directed the film *Hell's Angels*.

1933 He worked as an airline pilot. (He changed his name).

1935 He built a plane. He broke the world air-speed record. (He flew at 352 m.p.h.)

1937 President Roosevelt gave him a special aviation award.

1938 He flew round the world in 91 hours (a new world record).

1942 He designed and manufactured war planes.

1943 He designed a new bra for film-star Jane Russell.

1947 He started T.W.A. (Trans World Airlines). He crashed a new war-plane. He nearly died. In hospital, he designed a new bed. He flew a new 700-seat passenger plane.

1948 He bought RKO Film Studio.

1954 He sold RKO.

1957 He sold TWA for $546,000,000. He married Jean Peters.

1958 He retired from public life.

1966 He went to Las Vegas. He bought a lot of casinos, clubs, and hotels. (He didn't smoke, drink or gamble.)

1971 He divorced Jean Peters.

1972 He gave $100,000 to President Nixon for the 1972 Election.

5th April 1976 Hughes died in Acapulco. He left $2,000,000,000.

54 The boss and the secretary

Mr Gibbon Well, Miss Smith . . . this is a change! I usually have water with my meals, you know.

Miss Smith Yes, Mr Gibbon, but tonight we're having champagne!

Mr Gibbon Please don't call me Mr Gibbon. My friends always call me Horace.

Miss Smith All right . . . Horace . . . and we're having fillet steak!

Mr Gibbon Isn't it wonderful! I normally have egg and chips on Mondays . . . you see, my wife doesn't like restaurants.

Miss Smith Oh, your wife . . . what's she doing now?

Mr Gibbon Er . . . she's watching television at home. What perfume are you wearing, Miss Smith?

Miss Smith Please . . . call me Dorothy. I'm wearing "Night of Passion".

Mr Gibbon It's lovely. My wife never wears perfume . . .

Miss Smith I don't always wear it, but this is a special occasion.

Mr Gibbon Of course it is. I never come to restaurants like this. Dorothy, I want to ask you something.

Miss Smith Oh, Horace, go on . . . I'm enjoying this evening so much.

Mr Gibbon Well . . . it's difficult.

Miss Smith Please . . . ask me.

Mr Gibbon Well, you know we've got a lot of work at the office. . . .

Miss Smith Yes?

Mr Gibbon Well, can you work on Saturdays until we finish it?

Miss Smith Oh!

Questions

What's he drinking tonight?
What does he usually drink?
What's he eating tonight?
What does he usually eat on Mondays?
Is Miss Smith wearing perfume tonight?
Does she always wear perfume?

Exercise

He usually drinks water.
tonight/champagne
But tonight he's drinking champagne.

1 He usually eats eggs.
   tonight/steak
2 He usually drinks beer.
   tonight/whisky
3 He usually smokes cigarettes.
   tonight/cigars
4 He usually eats at home.
   tonight/in a restaurant

55 An accident

Two cars were going along Cambridge Street. An Englishman was driving a Rolls-Royce, and a foreign student was driving a V.W. The Englishman was driving slowly and carefully. The student wasn't driving carefully . . . he was looking at a girl. She was walking along the street. She was wearing a short skirt, and she was carrying a handbag. The traffic-lights were green. A dog was sitting beside the traffic-lights. A cat was sitting on the opposite corner.

The dog was thinking about a bone.

Suddenly the dog saw the cat.

It ran across the road.

The English driver saw the dog.

He braked quickly.

The V.W. crashed into the Rolls-Royce.

The girl saw the accident.

She ran to a telephone box.

The police came immediately.

56 An investigation

Last night at 9.18 the Director of a school was walking from his office to his car when he was attacked from behind. The attacker hit the Director on the head. The police think the attacker was a student . . . maybe a girl student! The police are going to interview every student in the school.

Questions

When did it happen?
What time did it happen?
Where was the Director going?
Where was he coming from?
Did the attacker hit him?
Where did the attacker hit him?
What do the police think?
Who's coming to the school later today?
What are they going to do?

A policeman interviewed the Director at the hospital last night:

Policeman Now, Mr Snow . . . what can you remember about the attack?
Mr Snow Well, I was working late yesterday evening. . . .
Policeman What time did you leave your office?
Mr Snow About quarter past nine.
Policeman Are you sure?
Mr Snow Oh, yes . . . I looked at my watch.
Policeman What did you do then?
Mr Snow Well, I locked the door . . . and I was walking to my car, when somebody hit me on the head.
Policeman Did you see the attacker?
Mr Snow No, he was wearing a stocking over his head.
Policeman Tell me, Mr Snow . . . how did you break your leg?
Mr Snow Well, when they were putting me into the ambulance, they dropped me!

Questions

Where's Mr Snow now?
What's he doing?
What's the policeman doing?
What was Mr Snow doing at nine o'clock yesterday?
What time did he leave his office?
Is he sure?
Ask "Why?"
What did he lock?
When did the attacker hit him?
Did he see the attacker?
Ask "Why not?"
Did Mr Snow break his arm?
Ask "What?"
Ask "When?"

57 A photograph album

Jenny's 26. She's a teacher. She's in class now.

Jenny Now, Martin . . . can you swim?

Martin Yes, I can . . . I could swim when I was five.

Jenny Could you?

Martin Yes, Miss . . . could you swim when you were five?

Jenny I could swim when I was three.

Martin Really, Miss? Could you read and write when you were three?

Jenny No, Martin . . . of course I couldn't!

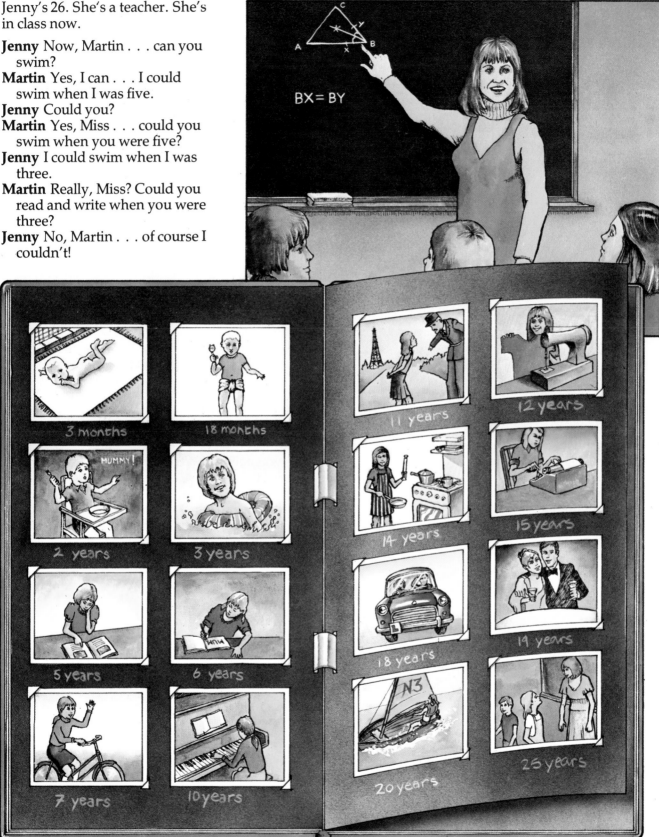

Exercise

When Jenny was ten, she could play the piano, and she could ride a bicycle. But she couldn't speak French, and she couldn't sew.

Now write ten sentences:
When I was ten, I could read.
When I was ten, I couldn't speak English.

58 A spy story

M This is a very important mission, 006.

006 What must I do?

M You must go to Moscow on tonight's plane.

006 Ah, Moscow! I've got a girlfriend there!

M We know that . . . but you mustn't visit her!

006 Where must I stay?

M You must go to the Airport Hotel, stay in your room and wait.

006 Which passport must I use?

M Your Swiss passport . . . and you must speak Swiss-German all the time. They mustn't know your nationality.

006 What must I take with me?

M Well, you mustn't carry your gun . . . but take a lot of warm clothes. Good luck, 006!

Questions

Is it an important mission?
Must he go to Moscow?
Ask "When?" Ask "How?"
Who mustn't he visit in Moscow?
Must he stay in a hotel?
Ask "Which hotel?"
Must he stay in his room?
What must he do there?
Which passport must he use?
Must he speak English?
Ask "What?" Ask "Why?"
What must he take with him?
What mustn't he take with him?

X Now, Olga. You must check into the Airport Hotel tonight.

Olga Must I reserve a room?

X No, you needn't. We reserved one for you . . . next to the British agent's room.

Olga Must I stay in my room?

X No, you needn't stay in your room, but you must stay in the hotel.

Olga Must I . . . be nice to him?

X No, you needn't . . . but you must discover why he's here.

Olga Must I contact you every day?

X No, you mustn't! It's too dangerous for you.

Olga Why?

X Because 006 is a very dangerous man.

Questions

Must she check into the hotel tonight?
Must she reserve a room?
Must she stay in her room?
Must she stay in the hotel?
Must she be nice to 006?
What must she discover?
Must she contact 'X' every day?
Ask "Why not?"

Exercise

I'm on a diet, so
I mustn't eat bread.
I mustn't drink beer.
I mustn't go
everywhere by car.

I'm a millionaire, so
I needn't work.
I needn't save my
money.
I needn't worry about
inflation.

Write six true
sentences.
Begin
I mustn't • • • •
I needn't • • • •

59 Everyday Conversation

M Bournemouth 18233.
N Hello. This is Tom Piper here. Is Mary there?
M Hang on a minute. I'll see.
N O.K.
M Hello. I'm sorry, but Mary's out.
N Oh! Could you take a message?
M Yes, of course. Just a minute. I need a pen.

18233
50079
61443
88220
74597

Tom Piper
Guy Black
Alan Heath
Nigel Thatcher
Chris Owen

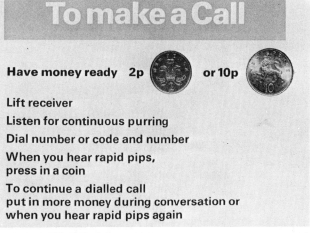

O Hello. Directory Enquiries. Can I help you?
P Yes. Can I dial direct to Zurich?
O Yes sir, you can.
P What's the S.T.D. code number, please?
O It's 010411.
P Thank you.

Zurich/010411
Paris/010331
Rome/010396
Chicago/0101312
Teheran/0109821

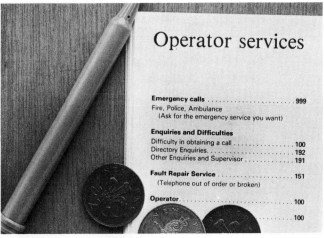

Q Hello. Radio Taxis.
R I'd like a taxi, please.
Q When do you want it?
R As soon as possible.
Q Where are you?
R On the corner of London Road and Strouden Street.
Q Where do you want to go?
R The station.
Q What's the name?
R Johnson. Mr Johnson.
Q O.K. Thank you.

the station
the airport
the hospital
the bus station
the ABC cinema

Mr Johnson
Mrs Taylor
Miss Baker
Dr Steele

S Hello. International Service. Can I help you?
T Yes, please. I'd like to make a three-minute call to Madrid.
S What's the number, please?
T Madrid 65.43.21.
S What's your number, please?
T Oxford 56767.
S Please put £1.56 in the box and I'll call you back.
T Thank you.

Madrid 654321
Lisbon 974483
Athens 107233
Vienna 449505
Brussels 1678901

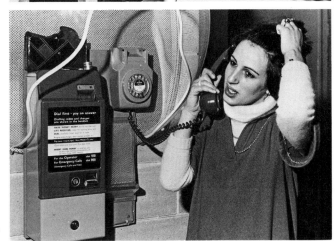

60 Another personal letter

> 13, rue Pigalle,
> Montmartre,
> Paris.
> August 16th 1977
>
> Dear John,
> Last weekend I went on an excursion to Versailles. I went with some students in my class. I got up at six o'clock on Saturday and met the other students at the station. In the morning we visited the Palace. It was very interesting. We saw Louis XIV's bedroom. We had lunch in a little café and I drank a lot of wine. In the afternoon we sat in the sun for an hour and walked through the gardens. I met a very interesting Frenchman with a big moustache. I didn't practise my French very much because he spoke English all the time.
> Did you have a nice weekend? I miss you a lot. Love, Mary.

Dear   John,
       Anne,
       Father,
       Mother,

Last	Monday	I went	on an excursion	to	Windsor.	I went with	my girlfriend.	I got up
	night		*on a trip*		*Cambridge.*		*some friends.*	
	weekend				*Stratford.*		*my boyfriend.*	

	early	and met	her	at the	station.	In the morning we visited	the castle.
	at seven o'clock		*him*		*school.*		*the village.*
	late		*them*		*bus station.*		*the town.*

It was very	interesting.	We saw	the river.	We had lunch in	a restaurant	and I drank
	boring.		*the university.*		*a pub*	
	beautiful.		*the old town.*		*a cafeteria*	

a lot of tea.	In the afternoon we sat	in a garden	and walked	through the park.	I met a very
some beer.		*by the river*		*around the town.*	
too much wine.		*in the park*		*along the river.*	

interesting	Englishman	with	blue eyes.	I didn't practise my English because	he	spoke	Spanish
handsome	*English girl*		*a beard.*		*she*		*Arabic*
beautiful			*long hair.*				*Japanese*

| all the time. Did you have a | nice weekend? | I miss you a lot. |
| | *good week?* | |

    Love,

61 On the moon

Phil Strongarm, the American astronaut has landed on the moon. He's speaking to Mission Control now:

Mission Control Hello, Phil . . . can you hear me?

Strongarm Yes, I can hear you clearly.

Mission Control What are you going to do next?

Strongarm I'm going to open the door.

Mission Control Hello, Phil . . . What are you doing now?

Strongarm I'm opening the door.

Mission Control Phil! Have you opened the door?

Strongarm Yes, I've opened the door. I can see the moon! It's fantastic!

Exercise

1 What's he going to do?
He's going to climb down the ladder.

What's he doing?
He's climb*ing* down the ladder.

What has he done?
He's climb*ed* down the ladder.

2 What's he going to do?
He's going to place the flag.

. . . ?
. . . .

. . . ?
. . . .

3 What's he going to do?
He's going to close the door.

. . . ?
. . . .

. . . ?
. . . .

62 Where's he gone?

Beryl Hello, Janet . . . what's the matter?

Janet It's my husband . . . he's gone!

Beryl Gone? Where's he gone?

Janet He's gone to Paris.

Beryl Has he gone on business?

Janet No, he hasn't gone on business. He's gone with Dorothy.

Beryl Dorothy? Who's Dorothy?

Janet She's his secretary.

Beryl Is he coming back?

Janet I don't know.

Paul Can you lend me £5?

Bill Sorry, I can't . . . I haven't been to the bank today.

Paul Oh dear . . . I haven't been either, and I need some money. It's too late now . . . it's four o'clock.

Bill Why don't you ask Peter?

Paul Oh, has he been to the bank?

Bill Yes, he has. He always goes on Mondays.

Exercise

 He's *been to the* bank.

 She . . . shops.

 They . . . church.

 He . . . hairdresser.

 She's *gone to* Paris.

 They . . . London.

 He . . . hospital.

 He . . . on business.

63 Everyday Conversation

U Oh, dear!
V What's wrong?
U I can't find my pen.
V Really!
U You mustn't laugh . . . it isn't funny.
V Oh, yes it is.
U Is it? Why?
V It's in your hand!
U Oh, yes.

pen
pencil
address book
diary

in your hand
in your pocket
on your desk
under your elbow

W Are you a foreigner?
X Pardon?
W ARE-YOU-A-FOREIGNER?
X You needn't shout. I'm not deaf.
W Oh, I'm sorry.
X That's all right. I just didn't understand. What does 'foreigner' mean?

foreigner
tourist
student
holiday-maker
teacher

Y Be careful!
Z Why?
Y I've just painted the door.
Z It's all right . . . I haven't touched it.
Y Haven't you? What's that on your arm?

door
shelf
desk
chair
wall

arm
hand
leg
shoulder
elbow

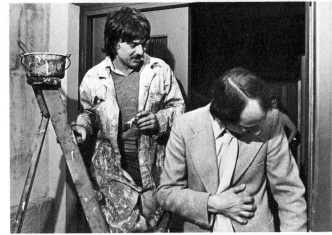

A I'm bored.
B Well, do something!
A What, for example?
B Wash your hair.
A I've already washed it.
B Brush your shoes.
A I've already brushed them.
B Why don't you clean your room?
A I've already cleaned it.
B Well, . . . perfect your English!
A Hmm. . . .

wash your hair
finish your homework
brush your shoes
iron your clothes
clean your room
telephone your friend
perfect your English
study your English

64 Town and Country

Chris Stan! I've got a new job! I'm going to live in London!

Stan Are you? Oh, I lived in London five years ago.

Chris Did you like it?

Stan Not very much.

Chris Why not?

Stan Well, there were too many people, and there was too much noise.

Chris Oh, I love crowds and noise!

Stan Well, I don't . . . and I don't like pollution.

Chris What do you mean?

Stan Oh, there isn't enough fresh air in London.

Chris But there are a lot of parks.

Stan Yes, I know . . . and people sleep in them!

Chris Why?

Stan Because there isn't enough accommodation . . . there aren't enough flats and houses.

Chris Well, I still prefer big cities.

Stan But why?

Chris I was born in a small country village. It was too quiet.

Stan You were lucky!

Chris I don't think so. There wasn't much to do. That's why young people go to London.

Stan But London's too expensive for young people.

Chris But they still go . . . they want excitement.

Stan Hmm . . . I don't want excitement. I just want a quiet life, that's all.

Exercise

In London

There's too much noise.
There isn't enough fresh air.
There are too many people.
There aren't enough flats.

In the World

1 . . . pollution.
2 . . . oil.
3 . . . people.
4 . . . doctors.

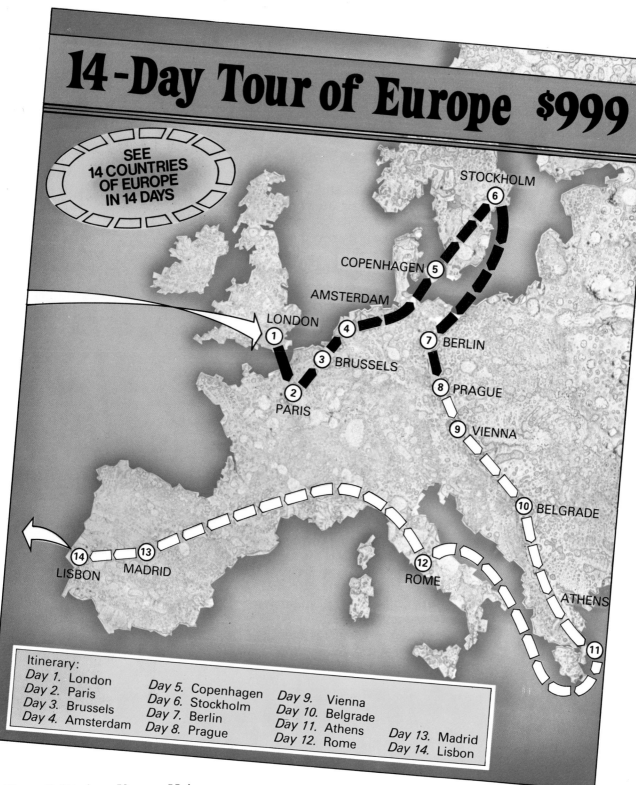

14-Day Tour of Europe $999

SEE 14 COUNTRIES OF EUROPE IN 14 DAYS

STOCKHOLM ⑥
COPENHAGEN ⑤
AMSTERDAM
LONDON ①
④
③ BRUSSELS
② PARIS
⑦ BERLIN
⑧ PRAGUE
⑨ VIENNA
⑩ BELGRADE
⑫ ROME
⑪ ATHENS
⑭ LISBON ⑬ MADRID

Itinerary:
Day 1. London
Day 2. Paris
Day 3. Brussels
Day 4. Amsterdam
Day 5. Copenhagen
Day 6. Stockholm
Day 7. Berlin
Day 8. Prague
Day 9. Vienna
Day 10. Belgrade
Day 11. Athens
Day 12. Rome
Day 13. Madrid
Day 14. Lisbon

Elmer Colt is from Kansas. He's on a 14-day tour of Europe. The tour started in London. At the moment he's in Prague. It's the eighth day of the tour. He's already been to seven countries and stayed in the capital cities.

He's never been to Europe before, and he's already seen a lot of new places. He's done a lot of interesting things . . . and the tour hasn't finished yet.

Exercise 1

Elmer's been to London, but he hasn't been to Vienna yet.
Write four sentences about Elmer.

Exercise 2

I've been to Paris, but I haven't been to London yet.
Write four sentences about yourself.

66 A call from home

KANSAS

PRAGUE

Mrs Colt Hello . . . Elmer? . . . Is that you?
Elmer Yes, Momma.
Mrs Colt Where are you now, Elmer?
Elmer I've just arrived in Prague, Momma.
Mrs Colt You haven't sent me any postcards yet.
Elmer Yes, I have . . . I've sent one from every city.
Mrs Colt Have you been to Paris yet, Elmer?
Elmer Yes, I have.
Mrs Colt Have you been to Vienna yet?
Elmer No, I haven't. We're going to Vienna tomorrow.

Mrs Colt Elmer! Are you still there?
Elmer Yes, Momma.
Mrs Colt How many countries have you seen now, Elmer?
Elmer Well, this is the eighth day, so I've already seen eight countries.
Mrs Colt Have you spent much money, Elmer?
Elmer Yes, Momma, I've bought a lot of souvenirs . . . and I want to buy some more. Can you send me a thousand dollars?
Mrs Colt All right, Elmer.

Mrs Colt Elmer, are you listening to me?
Elmer Yes, Momma.
Mrs Colt Have you taken many photographs, Elmer?
Elmer Yes, Momma, I've taken a lot. I've used three rolls of film.
Mrs Colt Have you met any nice girls yet, Elmer?
Elmer Oh, yes, Momma . . . there's a girl from Texas on the tour. We've done everything together.
Mrs Colt Elmer! Elmer! Are you still there, Elmer?

Exercise 1

postcards
How many postcards *has he sent?*
He's sent one from every city.

Write questions
and answers with:
1 capitals
2 money
3 souvenirs
4 photographs
5 rolls of film

Exercise 2

Have you ever bought a souvenir?
Yes, I have.
No, I haven't.

Answer these questions:
Have you ever seen the Queen?
Have you ever been to Paris?
Have you ever sent a postcard?
Have you ever spent a lot of money on a holiday?
Have you ever met an Englishman?
Have you ever taken photographs on a holiday?

67 Have you ever . . .?

A Have you ever studied a language before?
B Yes, I have.
A Oh, which one did you study?
B I studied French at school.

at school
at college
at evening classes
at home

C Have you ever been to a wedding?
D Yes, I have.
C Whose wedding was it?
D It was my brother's.

brother's
sister's
cousin's
friend's

E Have you ever seen a fire?
F Oh, yes, I have.
E When did you see it?
F I saw one in Manchester in 1976.

in 1975
in 1969
in 1977
in 1973

G Have you ever drunk too much?
H Yes . . . I have.
G Where did you drink too much?
H I drank too much at my brother's wedding.

at a wedding
at a party
at a dinner party
at a night club

I Have you ever eaten at the Royal Hotel?
J Yes, I have.
I When did you eat there?
J Mary and I ate there two months ago.

at the Royal Hotel
at the Station Hotel
at the Hong Kong Restaurant
at the Taj Mahal Restaurant

K Have you ever had flu?
L Yes, I have.
K When did you have it?
L I had it last winter.

last spring
last summer
last autumn
last winter

M Have you ever broken a bone?
N Yes, I have.
M What did you break?
N I broke my leg.

leg
arm
finger
shoulder

68 Comparisons

Canada (January) −20° C

Greenland −32° C

Canada's cold, but *Greenland's colder*.

Bermuda 35° C

Saudi Arabia 40° C

Bermuda's hot, but • • • •

Tommy   Billy

Tommy's older than Billy; so Billy's younger than Tommy.

Make sentences using these words:
tall/short
light/heavy
fat/thin
small/big

Canada's large, but the • • • •

Canada — 10,032,485 square km.

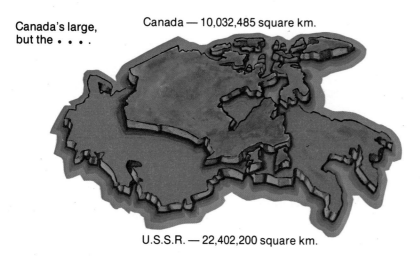

U.S.S.R. — 22,402,200 square km.

Layford School

Tommy Jones.

English: A
Maths: A
History: E
Geography: C
French: C
Science: B

Average: "C"

Layford School

Billy Jones.

English: A+
Maths: B
History: D
Geography: B
French: B
Science: E

Average: "B"

In Maths, Tommy's better than Billy; so Billy's worse than Tommy.

Make sentences about:
English/History/Geography/French/Science.

England   750 mm rain per year

Bangla Desh   3000 mm rain per year

England's wet, but • • • •

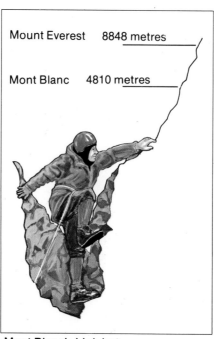

Mount Everest   8848 metres

Mont Blanc   4810 metres

Mont Blanc's high but • • • •

A car's more expensive than a motorcycle but a motorcycle's less comfortable than a car.

Make sentences using these words:
comfortable/dangerous/economical.

69 A hard life

Jerry Floyd is talking to his grandfather about his new job:

"It's terrible, granddad. I have to get up at seven o'clock because I have to catch the bus to work. Because I'm new, I have to make the tea. I have to work hard . . . I'm only happy at weekends: I don't have to work then."

Questions

Does he have to get up at 6 o'clock?
Does he have to get up at 7 o'clock?
Does he have to catch the train?
Does he have to catch the bus?
Does he have to make the coffee?
Does he have to make the tea?
Does he have to work hard?
Does he have to work on Saturday?

His grandfather isn't very sympathetic:

"I had to start work when I was 14. I lived in South Wales, and there wasn't much work. I had to be a coal miner. We had to work twelve hours a day. We didn't have to work on Sundays . . . but we had to work the other six days of the week.

Questions

Did he have to start work at 15, or did he have to start work at 14?
Did he live in North Wales, or did he live in South Wales?
Did he have to be a teacher, or did he have to be a coal miner?
Did he have to work 8 hours a day, or did he have to work 12 hours a day?
Did he have to work 5 days a week, or did he have to work 6 days a week?
Did he have to work on Sundays?

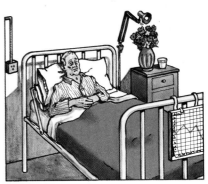

"When I was eighteen, the First World War started. I joined the army. I had to wear a uniform, and I had to go to France. A lot of my friends died. We had to obey the officers, and we had to kill people.

Questions

When did the First World War start?
How old was he then?
What did he have to join?
What did he have to wear?
Where did he have to go?
How many of his friends died?
Who did he have to obey?
What did he have to do?

"When I was sixty, I had to go into hospital because of the dust from the mines. It was the only quiet time in my life . . . I didn't have to work, I didn't have to earn money.

Questions

Did he have to go into hospital?
When did he have to go into hospital?
Why did he have to go into hospital?
Did he have to work in hospital?
Did he have to earn money?

"I retired when I was sixty-five. Nowadays I don't work and I don't have to get up early. But I have to live on my pension, and life is still difficult. I don't feel sorry for you."

Questions

Did he retire at 60?
Ask "When?"
What doesn't he have to do now?
Does he earn money now?
What does he live on?
Is life easy for him now, or is it difficult?
Does he feel sorry for his grandson?

70 Comparisons

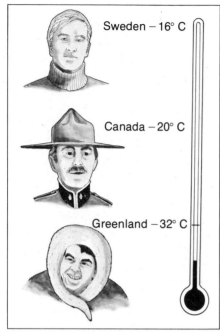

Sweden – 16° C

Canada – 20° C

Greenland – 32° C

They are all cold, *but Greenland's the coldest.*

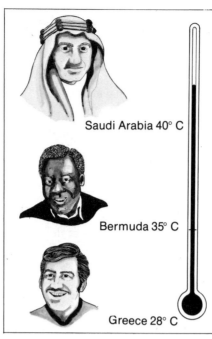

Saudi Arabia 40° C

Bermuda 35° C

Greece 28° C

They are all hot, • • • •

MARY
ANNE
MARGARET

Mary's the tallest.
Margaret's the shortest.

Make sentences using these words:
light/heavy
old/young
fat/thin
small/big

They are all large,
• • • •

China
9,561,000 square km.

Canada
10,032,485 square km.

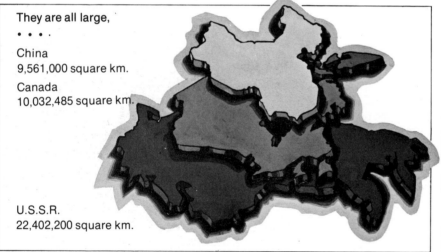

U.S.S.R.
22,402,200 square km.

Seacombe School Report			
	Mary	Anne	Margaret
English	A	B+	B
Maths	D	D–	E
History	A+	A	B
Geography	C–	D	E
French	A	B–	A+
Science	E	D	C–
Biology	B	A	B–
Music	D–	E	D+

In English, Mary's the best.
In Maths, Margaret's the worst.
Make sentences about: Maths/History/Geography/French/Science/Biology/Music.

England — 750 mm rain per year

Vietnam — 2,500 mm per year

Bangla Desh — 3,000 mm rain per year

They are all wet, • • • •

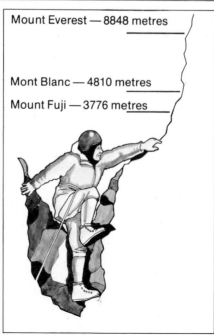

Mount Everest — 8848 metres

Mont Blanc — 4810 metres

Mount Fuji — 3776 metres

They are all high, • • • •

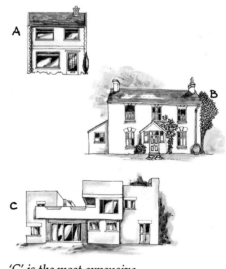

A

B

C

'C' is the most expensive.
'A' is the least expensive.
Make sentences using these words:
modern/beautiful/interesting.

71 Brutus Cray — the Greatest

Brutus Cray I'm the greatest!
Reporter You were the greatest, Brutus . . . but you're ten years older than Joe Freezer.
Cray Joe Freezer! I'm not afraid of Joe Freezer!
Rep. Really?
Cray Listen! I've beaten him twice, and I'm going to beat him again.
Rep. Are you sure?
Cray Sure? Of course I'm sure.
Rep. Some people say he's better than you.
Cray Listen! I've beaten all the best boxers, and Joe Freezer's one of the worst!
Rep. Yes, but he's better than he was.
Cray Listen! I'm stronger, faster, fitter and more intelligent than him!
Rep. Yes, but he KO'ed Len Korton two months ago.
Cray Len Korton. I've KO'ed him three times!
Rep. O.K., O.K., Brutus. Are you going to retire after this fight?
Cray Retire? No. I've been the champion for ten years . . . and I'm going to stay the champion for another ten.
Rep. Joe Freezer doesn't think so!
Cray Joe Freezer? Joe Freezer's the ugliest man in the world . . . after tonight he's going to need a new face!

Questions

Is Brutus older than Joe Freezer?
Is he afraid of Joe Freezer?
Has he beaten him before?
Ask "How many times?"

Has he beaten other boxers?
Ask "Which boxers?"
Is Freezer worse than he was, or better than he was?

Has Freezer beaten Len Korton?
Ask "When?"
Is Brutus going to retire?
How long has he been the champion?

Exercise

A Joe Freezer/ugly
B He/Brutus Cray
C He/the world

Write sentences like this:

A Joe Freezer is very ugly.
B He's uglier than Brutus Cray.
C He's the ugliest man in the world.

a Rockefeller/rich
b He/the teacher
c He/the world

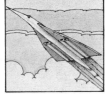

a Concorde/fast
b It/a Boeing
c It/the world

a Mount Everest/high
b It/Mont Blanc
c It/the world

a Rolls-Royce/comfortable
b It/Mini
c It/the world

a Brutus Cray/good
b He/Joe Freezer
c He/the world

72 George and Brenda

George Will you marry me, darling?
Brenda Of course I will.
George Is that a promise?
Brenda Of course it is . . . I love you.

Brenda Oh, darling, I feel terribly tired!
George Well, sit down. I'll do the washing-up.
Brenda Oh, thank you darling . . . and I'm thirsty.
George All right, I'll make you a cup of tea.

Brenda George! Have you mended that plug yet?
George No, I haven't.
Brenda Well, will you do it today?
George Yes, I'll do it now. Where's the screwdriver?
Brenda I don't know.
George Well, I can't find it. I'll do it tomorrow.

Brenda Oh, George . . . we haven't got much for dinner.
George That's all right. Shall we eat out?
Brenda Oh, yes! Where shall we go?
George Let's go to that new Italian Restaurant!

Brenda George!
George Yes, dear.
Brenda You're drunk! Shall I drive?
George No, I'm O.K. I'll drive.
Brenda No, you won't. Give me the keys!

73 Everyday Conversation

C What's the matter? Why has the bus stopped?
D There's been an accident.
C Has there? Again?
D Yes, there have been three here this week.
C Yes, I know. And it's only Wednesday.
D Yes. It's the most dangerous corner I've ever seen.

this week
this month
this year
this summer
this winter

corner
bend
hill
roundabout
junction

E Look at that girl!
F What about her?
E Look at her dress!
F What about it?
E It's the same as mine! That's what!
F No, it isn't. It's different from yours.
E Is it?
F Yes. Hers is shorter than yours.

dress
skirt
coat
raincoat
jacket

shorter
cheaper
longer
more expensive

G Are you a new student?
H No, I'm not.
G Oh. How long have you been here?
H As long as you.
G Why haven't I seen you?
H I've been ill.

student
teacher
typist
secretary

ill
sick
away
on holiday

I Can I borrow £10?
J Why don't you go to the bank?
I My cheque hasn't arrived yet.
J Well, I'm sorry, but I'm broke.
I What can I do?
J Ask George. He's as rich as Rockefeller.

£10
$10
£5
$5

George
Stuart
Jeffrey
Charles
Arthur

74 Something, nothing, anything, everything

A I want some seats for Tuesday night. Are there any left?
B No, there are no seats left. Every seat is reserved.

C Doctor, I think there's something in my eye. Everything looks funny.
D Let me have a look . . . I can't see anything . . . No, I'm sure there's nothing there.

E There's somebody in the other office!
F I didn't hear anybody.
E Well, just have a look . . .
F . . . No, there's nobody there. Everybody's gone home.

G What are you looking for?
H My pen. It's somewhere in this room!
G Where have you looked?
H I've looked everywhere . . . and I can't find it anywhere!

Exercise

1 There's *something* in my soup.
What is it?
There's *somebody* in the other room.
Who is it?

2 Is there anything in the fridge?
I'm hungry.
Is there • • • in the bathroom?
I want to brush my teeth.

3 There isn't anything in the fridge.
There isn't • • • in the bathroom.
It's empty.

4 Everything's expensive. Nothing's cheap.
• • • 's in the garden. • • • 's here.

Study this

some	any?	no/not . . . any	every
something	anything?	nothing/not . . . anything	everything
somebody	anybody?	nobody/not . . . anybody	everybody
someone	anyone?	no one/not . . . anyone	everyone
somewhere	anywhere?	nowhere/not . . . anywhere	everywhere

75 Four lives

Herbert Burke, James Stephens, Mary Foot, and Charlie Phillips all went to the same school. They left school in 1960, and they've had very different careers.

Herbert Burke became a politician ten years ago. He's very successful. He bought a country house five years ago, and bought a Jaguar at the same time. He's been a Member of Parliament for ten years. He's had his house and car for five years.

Questions

When did Herbert Burke become a politician?
When did he buy a country house?
When did he buy a Jaguar?
How long has he been a Member of Parliament?
How long has he had his house?
How long has he had his car?

Exercise

He's been there *since* 1969.
They've been there *for* five years.
Complete these in the same way:
1 She's had that watch . . . three weeks.

James Stephens is a criminal. He robbed a bank in 1971, and escaped to a Pacific island. He bought a luxury yacht the same year. He's still on the island. He's been there since 1971. He's had the yacht since 1971.

Questions

When did James rob a bank?
Where did he escape to?
What did he buy?
When did he buy it?
Where is he now?
How long has he been there?
How long has he had his yacht?

2 We've been here . . . January.
3 I've had my camera . . . two years.
4 They've been married . . . 1971.
5 He's had his car . . . two months.
6 John's been in London . . . March.

Mary Foot and Charlie Phillips fell in love at school. He gave her a ring when they left school. She wears it every day, and she's never taken it off. They got married in 1963 and they are still in love. They moved to Australia in 1968.

Questions

When did Mary and Charlie fall in love?
When did he give her the ring?
Has she ever taken it off?
When did they get married?
Are they still in love?
When did they move to Australia?
How long has she had the ring?
How long have they been married?
How long have they been in Australia?

76 A night out

77 The election result

It's midnight.
In a moment, the Mayor of Bamford is going to read the results of the General Election. Both of the candidates are on the balcony with the Mayor. Both of them are smiling, but neither of them are happy.
Both of them are wearing rosettes. One of them is the Labour candidate, and the other is the Conservative candidate. Neither of them have been Members of Parliament before.

The Mayor has just announced the result. The Labour candidate has won the election. Some of the crowd are pleased, but the others are angry. All of the Labour supporters are happy. All of them are shouting and cheering. The Conservative supporters are booing. None of them are smiling. The Conservatives haven't won an election in Bamford for many years. The Labour Party has won every election in the town since 1945.

Exercise

Example
One of them is a policeman.

 . . . nurse.

Both of them are policemen.

 . . . nurses.

Neither of them are policemen.

 . . . nurses.

Some of them are happy.

 . . . fat.

All of them are happy.

 . . . fat.

None of them are happy.

 . . . fat.

The Daily News

15p

Weather: fine

London: Wednesday May 20th

SENSATIONAL JEWEL ROBBERY
£50,000 STOLEN

There was a fifty thousand pound jewel robbery in central London yesterday. The thieves threw a stone through the window of Carbunkle & Company and stole necklaces, rings and watches worth £50,000. Mr Goldsmith, the manager of the shop, was working in his office when it happened. The police are looking for three men. The men drove away in a stolen Ford Cortina. The police have not found the getaway car yet.

Everest Expedition Fails

Three British climbers in the Himalayas wanted to reach the top of Mount Everest yesterday, but they failed because the weather has been too bad. They had to postpone the climb until next week. The weather has been the worst for two years.

Hollywood Divorce Case

Richard Taylor, the British actor, is going to divorce his wife, Liza Bertram. They have been married for thirteen years, and have lived in Hollywood since 1978. Several people have seen Taylor with film starlet Judy Bowes recently. He has been married four times. He refused to speak to our reporter yesterday.

Police Notice

Have you seen this girl?

Maria Roberts, a 15-year-old schoolgirl, left her home in Leeds last week and nobody has seen her since. She was wearing a blue raincoat, green trousers and black shoes. She has blonde hair blue eyes.
Please telephone:
0202-17414 with any information.

79 Everyday Conversation

K Can I help you?
L Yes, I want to send some flowers to my mother in Germany.
K What kind of flowers would you like?
L Well, what do you recommend?
K Well, roses are very nice at this time of the year.
L O.K. . . . a dozen roses, please.

roses
tulips
daffodils
carnations

a dozen (12)
half a dozen (6)
two dozen (24)
ten (10)

M Mrs Connor?
N Yes, Paul?
M This is a present for you.
N A present? What a lovely surprise! Shall I open it now?
M Yes, of course.
N Ooh! Chocolates! I love chocolates . . . Thank you, very much indeed!
M Thank *you*. You've been very kind.

chocolates
sweets
perfume
fruit

O I'd like to say goodbye to everybody.
P When are you leaving?
O Tomorrow morning.
P Let's meet for a coffee tonight.
O I'm afraid I can't.
P Oh . . . come on!
O No, really . . . I've got *so* much to do.

tomorrow morning
tomorrow afternoon
tomorrow evening
tomorrow night

Q It's been a lovely party. Thank you very much.
R But you can't go yet! The party's just beginning!
Q I'm sorry, but I must!
R Why?
Q Because I have to catch the last train.
R Don't be silly! I'll give you a lift. Where are you going?
Q Caracas!
R Oh!!

Caracas!
Tokyo!
Istanbul!
Rio!

80 A fourth letter

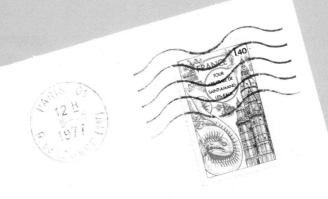

Mr. John Carter,
    ~~Nelson~~ Road,

                        13 rue Pigalle,
                        Montmartre,
                        Paris.
                        August 23rd, 1977

Dear John,

    I've missed you very much. I've been lonely this week because I haven't seen you for a month. I've learnt a lot of French this week ... I've worked hard. I haven't been out too much. Last night I had to do a lot of homework, and I'm tired today.

    Paris is smaller than London, but it's more interesting. I think it's the best city I've ever been to. There's too much traffic and there aren't enough restaurants with English food, but I like it. All of my teachers are very nice, and none of them speak English to me... so I have to speak French.

    Anyway, I must finish now. I'll write again soon... I promise.

    All my love,

                        Mary xxx

Dear John,
Mum,
Dad,
Mary,

I've missed	you	very much.	I've been	lonely	this week, because I
	home	*a lot.*		*sad*	
	the family	*quite a lot.*		*miserable*	

haven't seen you	for	a month.	I've learnt	a lot of	English	this week. I've worked
	since	*last month.*		*a little*	*French*	
		a long time.		*no*		

hard	this week. I haven't been out	much.	Last night I had to
a lot		*at all.*	
only a little		*many times.*	

study a lot,	and I'm	tired	today. London is	more expensive	than	Tokyo,
do a test,		*sleepy*		*cheaper*		*Rio,*
write a composition,				*smaller*		*Paris,*

but it's	more	interesting.	I think it's the	best	city I've ever	been to.	There	's
	less	*exciting.*		*worst*		*seen.*		*are*
		beautiful.				*visited.*		

too	much	traffic	and there aren't enough	restaurants	with	English food,
	many	*dogs*		*clubs*		*French wine,*
		pollution		*bars*		*German beer,*
		people		*discos*		*Spanish people,*

but	I	like	it.	All	of my teachers are very	good	and none of them speak
and		*love*		*None*		*beautiful*	
		hate		*Some*		*intelligent*	
						handsome	

Japanese	to me, so I have to speak English.	Well,	I	really must	finish now. I'll
Italian		*Anyway,*		*must*	
Portuguese				*have to*	
Arabic				*want to*	

write again	tomorrow,	. . . I promise.
	soon,	
	on Wednesday,	
	next week,	

All my love,

Yours,

Vocabulary

This vocabulary contains all the words in the student's book, and the number of the unit where they first occur.

A

a 1
about 15
Academy
  Award 53
accident 38
accommodation 64
across 25
action 12
actor 12
actress 12
address 19
address-book 63
afraid 47
after 26
afternoon 29
again 45
against 48
age 29
ago 51
agent 6
air 64
air-force 52
air-hostess 4
airport 4
album 57
all 28
all right 7
along 25
always 35
am 1
ambulance 56
American 1
an 3
and 1
angry 5
announce 77
another 23
any 6
anybody 74
anything 16
anyway 23
anywhere 74
apple 3
apple-pie 11
April 41
Arabic 14
are 1
area 52
arm 56
army 69
arrive 32
as 31
ash-tray 3
ask 22
asleep 47
astronaut 8
at 12
athletic 14

attack(v) 52
attacker 56
August 41
autumn 67
average 68
away 31

B

back 48
backache 39
bad 38
badly 38
baker 45
balcony 6
ballet 36
banana 10
bank 7
bath 5
bath-room 6
be(v) 12
beach 42
beard 29
beat(v) 71
beautiful 5
because 25
become 53
bed 3
bedroom 6
beef 11
beer 10
before 26
begin 52
behind 25
belt 24
bend 25
Ben Nevis 52
beside 5
best 40
best man 28
best wishes 20
better 68
between 25
bicycle 9
big 5
bill 19
billionaire 53
biography 53
Biology 70
birthday 44
biscuit 11
black 8
blonde 78
blouse 8
blue 8
boat 15
boiled 11
bomb(v) 52
bone 55
boo(v) 77
book 23

boot 31
boring 60
borrow 23
boss 9
both 28
bottle 6
bottom 78
box 22
boy 25
bra (brassiere) 53
brake(v) 55
brandy 19
Brazilian 20
bread 7
break(v) 52
breakfast 32
bride 28
bridesmaid 28
briefcase 9
bring 19
bring (back) 48
broke 16
brother 9
brown 8
brush(v) 63
build(v) 53
bullet 47
burn(v) 52
bus 3
(on) business 62
businessman 2
bus station 19
bus-stop 7
busy 20
but 14
butcher 45
butter 7
button 18
buy(v) 25
by 29, 60
bye 19

C

café 7
cafeteria 60
cake 7
call 4
call(v) 5
calmly 47
camera 5
can 14
Canada 1
canteen 33
Captain 8
car 3
cardigan 15
career 75
careful 63
carefully 38
carelessly 38
carrot 11
carry 22
case 4
case (legal) 78
cashier 25

casino 33
casserole 11
cassette 23
cassette-player 13
cassette-recorder 19
castle 60
cat 29
catch(v) 32
caviare 33
centigrade 68
central 41
certainly 7
chain 24
chair 3
champagne 27
champion 37
(a) change 54
change 31
change (v) 31
cheap 5
check into 58
cheer (v) 77
cheese 10
chemist 45
cheque 73
chess 29
chicken 10
Chinese 15
(a) chocolate 15
chocolate 18
Christmas 19
church 20
cigar 9
cigarette 17
cigar-lighter 13
cinema 20
class 20
classical 18
clean (v) 22
cleaner 4
clearly 61
clock 3
close (v) 12
club 21
coach 48
coal 69
coast 40
coat 18
cocktail-cabinet 13
code 59
coffee 11
coin 31
cold 5
(a) cold 39
college 67
colour 8
come 8
comfortable 13
company 36
competitor 34
complete (v) 29
composition 80

computer 29
computer-dating 29
concert 23
conductor 51
Conservative 77
contact 58
continuous 59
cook 4
cook (v) 14
cooker 6
corner 55
cornflakes 33
cotton 24
cough 51
could (request) 7
could (ability) 57
country 64
country-house 75
cousin 67
cowboy 22
crash (v) 49
cream 19
cricket 14
criminal 75
crowd 64
cry (v) 28
cup 3
cupboard 6
customer 11
Customs 17
Customs officer 17

D

daffodil 79
daily 78
dance 39
dance (v) 14
dancing 29
dangerous 58
Danish 43
dark 24
darling 26
date 29
daughter 11
day 23
Dear . . . 20
deaf 63
dear 22
December 41
declare 17
deep 68
degree 68
dentist 34
design 53
dessert 11
dial 59
diamond 24
diary 63
dictate 32
dictionary 23
did 44
die (v) 53

diet 15
different 73
difficult 22
dinghy 49
dinner 32
dinner-party 67
diploma 34
direct 59
direct (v) 53
director 12
Directory
  Enquiries 59
disco 20
discover (v) 58
dish 22
dislike 29
divorce 78
divorce (v) 53
do (v) 12
doctor/ Dr 8
does 30
dog 29
doing 21
dollar 53
done 61
door 3
double 7
down 2
dozen 79
draw 21
dress 5
dress (v) 32
(a) (drink) 15
drink (v) 11
drive (v) 14
driver 33
drop (v) 56
dry 70
dust 69

E

early 60
earn 69
ear-ring 24
Easter 35
eat 21
economical 31
egg 3
eighth 26
either 24
elbow 63
election 53
electric 13
elephant 48
eleventh 26
emergency 59
empty 5
end 47
engaged 30
engine 13
England 1
English 2
enjoy 47
enormous 33
enough 64

escape (v) 75
Europe 65
evening 18
ever 36
every 33
everybody 12
everything 16
everywhere 74
example 29
excitement 64
exciting 20
excellent 14
excursion 15
Excuse me! 2
expedition 78
expensive 5
eye 12

F

face 71
factory 16
fail (v) 78
fall (in love) (v) 75
family 8
famous 13
far 7
farmer 29
fashion 24
fashion-show 24
fast 13
fat 5
father 9
favourite 26
February 41
feel (sorry for) (v) 69
few 28
fifth 26
fight (v) 71
film 12
film director 12
find (v) 51
film star 12
fine 1
fine (weather) 78
finish (v) 40
fire (v) 47
fire 59
first 7
First World War 69
fish 49
fishing 29
fit 71
flag 61
flared 24
flower 28
flat 6
fly (v) 28
food 20
foot 39
football 14
football match 4
for 31
foreign 48

foreigner 63
for ever 28
for example 7
forget 19
fork 3
form 29
fourth 26
France 1
free 23
freezer 3
French 4
Frenchman 60
fresh 64
Friday 23
fridge 6
fried 11
friend 22
friendly 20
from 12
(in) front (of) 25
fruit 11
fruit salad 11
full 5
funny 63

G

gamble (v) 53
General Election 77
Geography 68
gentleman 34
get 19
getaway car 78
get into 28
get married 75
get up (v) 32
girl 56
girlfriend 25
give (v) 30
glass 3
glasses 9
go (v) 12
goal 52
going to do 27
gold 24
golf 29
good 6
Good afternoon 29
Good evening 4
Good morning 17
Goodnight 18
(a) good time 27
got (have got) 16
granddad 69
grandfather 69
grandparent 42
grandson 8
great! 16
green 8
grey 8
(bride)groom 28
group 50
guess (v) 34

guitarist 50
gun 47

H

hair 78
haircut 44
hairdresser 14
half 7
half-past 26
hamburger 10
hand 12
handbag 3
handsome 14
hang on 59
happen 56
happy 13
hard 38
hat 9
hate (v) 80
have (got) 14
he 1
head 56
hear (v) 59
heavy 5
Hello 1
help (v) 22
her (poss) 4
her (obj) 12
hers 18
Hi! 16
high 68
The Highlands 52
hill 73
him 12
his (poss) 4
his (pronoun) 18
history 68
hit (v) 56
hitch-hike (v) 48
hold (v) 28
holiday 2
holiday-maker 63
home 26
homework 22
honeymoon 28
horror 36
hospital 56
hot 5
hotel 4
hotel room 20
hour 39
house 3
housewife 8
How 31
How are you? 8
How about 15
How do you do? 8
How many? 10
How much? 7
How old? 29
hundred 17
hungry 5

(a) hurry 19
hurry (v) 47
husband 9

I

I 1
ice 7
ice-cream 3
identity card 17
I'd like 11
I'd love to 15
if 23
ill 73
immediately 55
important 34
in 6
indeed 79
inflation 58
information 15
inherit 53
insist 51
intelligent 71
interesting 20
international 19
International Service 59
interview 32
interview (v) 32
into 12
investigation 80
Iranian 2
iron 14
is 1
island 75
it (pronoun) 3
it (obj) 12
Italian 2
itinerary 65

J

jacket 8
January 41
Japan 1
Japanese 2
jar 10
jazz 29
jeans 8
jewel 78
jeweller 78
job 4
join (v) 69
jockey 37
joke (v) 27
journey 44
July 41
junction 73
June 29
juice 11
just 64

K

key 3
kill (v) 47

kilo 5
kilometre 68
kind 79
kiss (v) 12
kitchen 6
knife 3
know 30
K.O. 71

L

Labour 77
ladder 61
lady 34
lamb 11
landlady 39
language 14
language school 37
large 6
last 34
late 25
later 41
laugh (v) 47
laugh (n) 12
learn 40
least 70
leather 24
leave (v) 27
leave (money) (v) 53
lecture 44
left 28
leg 52
lemon 3
lend 62
let me see 43
letter 39
less 68
lie 25
life 16
lift (v) 19
lift (n) 59
light (adj) 5
light (n) 12
light (colour) 24
lighter 23
like (v) 29
likes (n) 29
like (What's it like?) 42
line 25
listen 47
litre 17
little 27
living room 6
lock 56
London 2
lonely 22
long 5
long (time) 73
look (v) 12
look at 12
look for 23
look into 12
lorry 3

lorry driver 33
lose (v) 51
lot 10
love 30
lovely 18
L.P. 18
Ltd. 36
luck 58
lucky 27
luggage 19
lunch 32
luxury 75

M

Madam 19
magazine 6
main course 11
make 13
man 13
manager 4
manufacture (v) 53
March 41
Market Research 36
married 20
marry 30
match 49
May 41
me 2
meal 54
mean (v) 64
measure (v) 43
meat 10
mechanic 4
medium 11
meet (v) 15
mend (v) 72
menu 11
message 59
metre 68
Metro 40
Mexican 2
microphone 12
midnight 77
milk 7
millimetre 68
million 53
millionaire 9
mine (pro) 18
miner 69
minus 68
miserable 80
Miss 8
miss (v) 47
mission 58
Mission Control 61
modern 31
moment 37
Monday 23
money 16
month 41
moon 44
more 18, 68

morning 17
morning suit 28
most 70
mother 9
mother-in-law 27
motorcycle 68
moustache 25
move (v) 12
M.P. 75
m.p.h. 53
Mr 4
Mrs 4
mushroom 10
music 29
my 4

N

name 4
nationality 2
near 7
nearly 45
necklace 24
need (v) 30
neither 77
never 35
new 5
news 26
newspaper 23
New York 2
next 27
nice 6
night 18
nightclub 21
nightdress 43
nil 52
ninth 26
No 1
no (not any) 74
nobody 74
noise 64
none 77
normal 44
normally 54
nose 74
not 1
note 31
nothing 33
notice 78
November 41
now 12
nowadays 35
nowhere 74
number 4
nylon 23

O

obey (v) 69
occasion 53
occasionally 35
occupation 29
ocean 49
o'clock 26
October 41

of 11
off 12
office 19
officer 69
often 35
Oh! 17
oil 7
oil-drilling company 53
old 5
omelette 11
O.K. 12
on 2
once 36
one 18
onion 10
only 49
opera 29
open (v) 12
operator 59
opposite 55
or 35
orange (colour) 8
orange (fruit) 3
orchestra 42
ordinary 32
other 60
our 4
ours 18
out 12
out of 25
outside 25
over 56
over there 4

P

paint (v) 63
pair 15
palace 52
pan 6
pardon 2
Paris 2
park (n) 60
party 23
pass (v) 7
passenger 53
passport 17
past 26
patient 52
pea 10
pen 3
pencil 63
pension 69
people 25
pepper 7
per cent 11
perfect (v) 63
perfume 17
personal 29
phone 7
phone (v) 22
photo-copy 46
photograph 29
piano 57
picnic 23

picture 20
piece 15
pilot 4
pineapple 49
pink 8
pint 7
pip 59
place 27
place (v) 61
plaice 11
plain 18
plan 6
plane 5
plate 3
play (v) 14
playboy 33
please 2
pleased 77
plug (n) 72
plus 68
police 52
policeman 4
politician 75
politics 29
pollution 64
poor 5
porter 4
Portuguese 11
post (v) 29
postcard 19
post office 7
possible 31
postpone 78
potato 11
pound 31
practise 22
prefer (v) 43
present (n) 28
President 52
press (v) 59
prison 27
private 42
problem 44
produce 53
professor 34
programme 26
promise (n) 72
promise (v) 80
protest (v) 52
pub 45
public 53
pull 47
pullover 15
purring 59
purse 51
put 12

Q

quarter past 26
quarter to 26
Queen 37
question 22
questionnaire 5
queue (v) 25
quickly 55

quiet 20
quite 36

R

racehorse 37
radio 3
rain 68
rainy 20
rapid 59
rarely 35
read (v) 21
really 14
rebel 50
receiver 59
reception (wedding) 28
reception (hotel) 4
receptionist 4
recommend 79
record 6
recreation 29
red 8
refuse (v) 78
regards 40
remember 80
rent 27
reply 32
reporter 32
repair (v) 31
rescue (v) 49
reserve (v) 46
reserved 20
rest (v) 21
restaurant 11
result 23
retire 24
return 44
reunion 8
rice 10
rich 5
ride (v) 37
right (opp. left) 28
right (opp. wrong) 43
ring 24
river 60
road 55
roast 11
rob 27
robbery 78
roll (bread) 45
roll (of films) 66
room 4
rose 79
rosé 11
rosette 77
round (prep) 18
royal 37
rubber 49
rugby 14
run (v) 12
rush (v) 47
Russian 2

S

sad 5
sail 57
salary 34
saloon 47
salt 7
same 73
sandwich 15
save (money) 58
scene 25
school 19
schoolboy 33
schoolgirl 78
Science 68
scientist 34
score (v) 52
screen 25
screwdriver 72
sea 28
seat 23
second 7
secretary 4
see 20
sell 53
send 19
sensational 78
sense 75
September 41
service 11
seventh 26
sew (v) 14
shampoo 79
shave (n) 44
she 1
shelf 3
sheriff 47
shine (v) 48
ship 49
shirt 8
shoe 8
shoot (v) 52
short 5
shorts 8
shoulder 63
shout (v) 25
show (v) 19
show (n) 24
shower 20
sick 73
sign (v) 46
signature 29
silly 79
silver 24
sing 14
single 20
sink 6
sister 9
sit 2
size 15
sixth 26
ski (v) 14
skirt 8
sleep (v) 21
sleepy 80

slow 13
slowly 38
small 5
smell (v) 74
smile (v) 12
smile (n) 28
smoke (v) 21
smoke (n) 25
snow (v) 52
so 31
soap 79
sober 76
sock 8
soda 7
sofa 6
some 9
somebody 56
someone 22
something 22
sometimes 35
somewhere 74
son 9
soon 30
sore 39
sore throat 39
sorry 19
sound (v) 74
soup 11
south 69
souvenir 66
Soviet Union 52
space 44
Spanish 2
speak (v) 14
special 54
speech 28
spell (v) 20
spend 28
spoon 3
sport 14
spring 67
spy 58
square 18
square km. 68
stadium 52
stand (v) 21
star 13
start (v) 12
starter 11
stay (v) 22
steak 11
steal 78
steps 25
stereo 13
still 64
stocking 56
stolen 78
stomach-ache 39
stone 78
stop (v) 51
story 47
stranger 63
street 40
striped 18
strong 5
STD 59

student 1
studio 12
study (v) 47
successful 75
sugar 2
suit 24
summer 67
sun 48
Sunday 23
sunglasses 24
sunny 20
supermarket 7
supper 44
supporter 77
sure 43
surname 20
surprise 8
survivor 49
sweet (n) 79
swim (v) 14
swim (n) 44
swimming pool 13
sympathetic 69

T

table 3
take 12
talk (v) 40
tall 5
taste (v) 74
taxi 3
tea 2
tea (meal) 27
teach 37
teacher 1
team 38
teenager 29
telegram 79
telephone (n) 6
telephone (v) 46
television 6
tell 31
temperature 39
tenth 26
terrible 16
terribly 72
terylene 24
test (n) 80
thank goodness! 51
thanks 1
thank you 2
thank you very much 4
that 3
the 3
theatre 20
their 4
theirs 18
them 12
then 32
there 4
these 3
they 1

thick 5
thief 78
thin 5
thing 20
think 31
third 7
thirsty 5
this 3
those 3
throat 39
throw 78
Thursday 23
ticket 17
time 15, 36
tired 5
title 23
to 12
tobacco 17
today 21
together 66
toilet 6
tomato 10
tomorrow 15
tonight 22
too (also) 24
too 43
top 78
top hat 28
touch (v) 63
tour 48
tourist 2
towards 47
towel 3
town 45
town hall 50
traditional 28
traffic-lights 35
train 3
transport café 33
travel (n) 30
travel (v) 34
trip 60
trousers 8
trouser suit 24
try on 15
T-shirt 8
tube 39
Tuesday 23
tulip 79
Turkish 43
turn off 12
turn on 12
twice 36
type (v) 14

U

ugly 5
umbrella 3
uncomfortable 44
under 6
understand 22
unhappy 22
uniform 34
United States 52

until 32
up 25
us 12
use (v) 58
usually 35

V

vanilla 18
V.A.T. 11
vegetable 11
Venezuelan 39
very 1
vicar 35
villa 28
village 60
vinegar 7
visa 17
visit (v) 36
vodka 17
vote (n) 77
vote (v) 77

W

wait (v) 25
waiter 4
wake up 32
walk (v) 12
Wales 52
wallet 51
want 30
warm 20
warplane 53
war 69
was 41
wash 22
wash up (v) 27
washing up (n) 72
water 10
watch (n) 3
watch (v) 22
we 2
weak 5
wear 24
weather 20
wedding 28
Wednesday 23
week 23
weekend 31
well 1
well (adv) 38
welcome (v) 32
well done 11
Wembley Stadium 52
were 41
wet 68
what 3
what about 22
what a pity 23
what colour 8
what kind 15
what make 13
what's the

matter 39
what time 15
wheel 13
when 15
where 1
which 12
which one 18
whisky 7
white 8
who 8
whose 9
why 25
wide 68
wife 8
will 72
win 51
window 3
wine 10
Winter 67
wishes 20
with 7
woman 25
wonderful 14
won't 72
woollen 24
word 22
work (v) 21
worker 16
work for 27
world record 53
worried 51
worry about 58
worst 70
worth 78
would 7, 15
write 48
wrong 43

XYZ

yacht 75
year 38
yellow 8
yes 1
yesterday 41
you 1
young 5
your 4
yours 18

Irregular verbs

Infinitive form	Past tense	Past participle	Infinitive form	Past tense	Past participle
be	was/were	been	lend	lent	lent
beat	beat	beaten	let	let	let
become	became	become	light	lit	lit
begin	began	begun	lose	lost	lost
bite	bit	bitten	make	made	made
break	broke	broken	mean	meant	meant
bring	brought	brought	meet	met	met
build	built	built	pay	paid	paid
burn	burnt	burnt	put	put	put
buy	bought	bought	read	read	read
catch	caught	caught	ride	rode	ridden
choose	chose	chosen	ring	rang	rung
come	came	come	run	ran	run
cost	cost	cost	say	said	said
cut	cut	cut	see	saw	seen
do	did	done	sell	sold	sold
drink	drank	drunk	send	sent	sent
drive	drove	driven	shine	shone	shone
eat	ate	eaten	shoot	shot	shot
fall	fell	fallen	show	showed	shown
feel	felt	felt	shut	shut	shut
fight	fought	fought	sing	sang	sung
find	found	found	sit	sat	sat
fly	flew	flown	sleep	slept	slept
forbid	forbade	forbidden	smell	smelt	smelt
forget	forgot	forgotten	speak	spoke	spoken
freeze	froze	frozen	spend	spent	spent
get	got	got	stand	stood	stood
give	gave	given	steal	stole	stolen
go	went	gone	swim	swam	swum
grow	grew	grown	take	took	taken
have	had	had	teach	taught	taught
hear	heard	heard	tear	tore	torn
hide	hid	hidden	tell	told	told
hit	hit	hit	think	thought	thought
hurt	hurt	hurt	throw	threw	thrown
keep	kept	kept	wake	woke	woken
know	knew	known	wear	wore	worn
learn	learnt	learnt	win	won	won
leave	left	left	write	wrote	written